Activism and Identity

The LGBTQ Movements on Xylon

Hassan Osei

ISBN: 9781779666161
Imprint: Press for Play Books
Copyright © 2024 Hassan Osei.
All Rights Reserved.

Contents

Introduction   1
The Importance of Activism and Identity in Imaginary Societies   1

Chapter One: The Dystopian Society of Xylon   13
The Historical Origins of Xylon   13
The LGBTQ Movements on Xylon   22

Chapter Two: The Utopian Society of Zephyria   33
The Founding Principles of Zephyria   33
The LGBTQ Movements on Zephyria   42

Chapter Three: The Post-Apocalyptic Society of Apolonia   53
The Collapse of Apolonia's Civilization   53
The LGBTQ Movements in Apolonia   62

Bibliography   65

Index   73

Introduction

The Importance of Activism and Identity in Imaginary Societies

Overview of the Different Imaginary Societies Explored in the Book

In this book, we explore three distinct imaginary societies: Xylon, Zephyria, and Apolonia. Each society serves as a unique lens through which we can examine the interplay between activism and identity, particularly within the context of LGBTQ movements. By analyzing these societies, we uncover the complexities and variances in how identity is constructed, challenged, and celebrated, and how activism emerges as a response to oppression and inequality.

Xylon: The Dystopian Society

Xylon represents a dystopian reality where societal structures are heavily influenced by authoritarian governance and systemic oppression. The historical origins of Xylon are rooted in a narrative of survival against adversity, where the emergence of a rigid caste system has led to the marginalization of various identities, particularly within the LGBTQ community.

Theoretical frameworks such as Foucault's concept of biopower ([?]) illustrate how power dynamics operate within Xylon, shaping identities and determining who is deemed acceptable or deviant. The LGBTQ movements in Xylon, characterized by both resistance and resilience, highlight the struggles against institutionalized discrimination and the quest for recognition. For instance, the formation of grassroots organizations like "Xylon Pride" showcases the community's efforts to reclaim their identities and advocate for rights amidst pervasive hostility.

Zephyria: The Utopian Society

In stark contrast to Xylon, Zephyria embodies the ideals of a utopian society, where principles of equality and social justice are foundational. The society's formation was driven by a collective desire to create an inclusive environment that celebrates diversity in all its forms. Theoretical perspectives, such as those proposed by Rawls in "A Theory of Justice" ([?]), serve as a backdrop for understanding the ethical frameworks that guide Zephyria's governance.

However, the utopian vision is not without its challenges. While LGBTQ rights are widely accepted, the society grapples with the complexities of maintaining this acceptance in the face of emerging tensions related to intersectionality. For example, the Zephyrian LGBTQ community has faced criticism for its inability to fully embrace the diverse experiences of all its members, particularly those from marginalized racial and socio-economic backgrounds. Such critiques reveal the limitations of utopian ideals when confronted with the realities of lived experiences.

Apolonia: The Post-Apocalyptic Society

Apolonia presents a post-apocalyptic scenario where the collapse of civilization has led to a re-evaluation of identity and community. The causes of this collapse—environmental degradation, resource depletion, and social fragmentation—have profound implications for how individuals navigate their identities in a world stripped of its former structures.

Theories of resilience and recovery, such as those articulated by Adger ([?]), inform our understanding of how the LGBTQ community in Apolonia has adapted to survive. The emergence of support networks and survival strategies illustrates the community's ingenuity in the face of adversity. For instance, the establishment of safe spaces known as "Haven Hubs" reflects a grassroots effort to create inclusive environments where LGBTQ individuals can find solidarity and support.

The fight for LGBTQ rights in Apolonia is fraught with challenges, as the community must contend with not only external threats but also internal divisions that arise from the struggle for recognition in a fractured society. The role of activism in this context is crucial, as it serves as a catalyst for rebuilding and redefining identities in a post-apocalyptic landscape.

Conclusion

Through the exploration of Xylon, Zephyria, and Apolonia, we gain valuable insights into the multifaceted nature of identity and activism within imaginary societies. These case studies not only highlight the struggles and triumphs of LGBTQ movements but also underscore the importance of understanding the historical and cultural contexts that shape these experiences. By examining these societies, we can better appreciate the complexity of activism and its potential to foster change in the face of oppression.

Understanding the Role of Identity in Imaginary Societies

The concept of identity is a multifaceted construct that plays a pivotal role in shaping the dynamics of imaginary societies. Identity not only influences individual experiences but also dictates the collective ethos of communities within these societies. This section delves into the theoretical frameworks surrounding identity, the challenges faced by individuals in asserting their identities, and the examples that illustrate these complexities in various imaginary contexts.

Theoretical Frameworks of Identity

Identity can be understood through various theoretical lenses, including social identity theory, intersectionality, and postmodern identity theory. According to [?], social identity theory posits that individuals derive a sense of self from their group memberships, which can include ethnicity, gender, sexuality, and other social categories. This theory highlights how social identities contribute to group cohesion and intergroup dynamics, often leading to in-group favoritism and out-group discrimination.

Intersectionality, a term coined by [?], further complicates our understanding of identity by emphasizing that individuals possess multiple, intersecting identities that can create unique experiences of privilege or oppression. For instance, a queer person of color in an imaginary society may face distinct challenges that differ from those experienced by a white cisgender individual, illustrating how the intersection of race, gender, and sexuality shapes one's lived experience.

Postmodern identity theory, as discussed by [?], argues that identity is fluid and constructed through social interactions rather than being a fixed essence. This perspective allows for a more nuanced understanding of identity in imaginary societies, where individuals may navigate multiple identities and adapt them according to the social context.

Challenges of Identity Assertion

In imaginary societies, individuals often encounter significant challenges when asserting their identities. These challenges can stem from cultural norms, institutional structures, and societal expectations that dictate acceptable forms of identity expression. For example, in the dystopian society of Xylon, rigid gender norms may suppress the expression of non-binary identities, leading to internal conflict and social ostracism.

Moreover, the concept of identity can be weaponized in these societies. [?] discusses how power dynamics shape identity formation, suggesting that those in power can impose identities that serve their interests while marginalizing others. In Xylon, the LGBTQ community may be subjected to surveillance and regulation, with their identities pathologized or criminalized, thus complicating their efforts to assert their identities authentically.

Examples from Imaginary Societies

The role of identity in imaginary societies can be illustrated through various case studies. In Xylon, the LGBTQ movements have emerged as a response to oppressive structures, with activists challenging the dominant narratives that seek to erase or distort their identities. Key figures, such as the activist group "Voices of Xylon," have utilized creative forms of protest, such as art and performance, to reclaim their identities and advocate for recognition and rights.

Conversely, in the utopian society of Zephyria, identity is celebrated, and diversity is woven into the fabric of social life. The Zephyrian LGBTQ community organizes vibrant festivals that honor different identities, fostering a sense of belonging and acceptance. This example demonstrates how a society's foundational principles can shape the expression and recognition of identity, leading to more inclusive outcomes.

In Apolonia, the post-apocalyptic context presents unique challenges for identity formation. As societal structures collapse, individuals must navigate the remnants of their previous identities while adapting to new realities. The LGBTQ community in Apolonia faces threats from both external forces and internal divisions, leading to the establishment of survival networks that prioritize mutual support. These networks exemplify the resilience of identity in the face of adversity, highlighting the importance of community in affirming and preserving diverse identities.

Conclusion

Understanding the role of identity in imaginary societies is crucial for comprehending the complexities of social dynamics and activism. Theoretical frameworks provide valuable insights into how identities are constructed and contested, while real-world examples illustrate the challenges and triumphs individuals face in asserting their identities. As we explore the intersections of identity and activism in the following chapters, we will continue to uncover the profound impact that identity has on shaping the narratives and futures of these imaginary societies.

The Impact of Activism on Imaginary Societies

Activism plays a pivotal role in shaping the social, political, and cultural landscapes of imaginary societies. By mobilizing individuals and communities around shared identities and causes, activism fosters change and challenges existing power structures. This section explores the multifaceted impact of activism within imaginary societies, drawing on theoretical frameworks and examples from the case studies presented in this book.

Theoretical Frameworks

To understand the impact of activism, we can draw from several theoretical perspectives, including social movement theory, intersectionality, and identity politics.

Social Movement Theory posits that social movements arise in response to perceived injustices and aim to promote social change. According to Tilly and Tarrow (2015), social movements are collective enterprises that seek to challenge the status quo. In imaginary societies, activism often emerges as a response to systemic oppression, providing a voice to marginalized groups. The success of these movements can be measured through various outcomes, including policy changes, shifts in public opinion, and the establishment of new social norms.

Intersectionality, a concept introduced by Crenshaw (1989), emphasizes the interconnectedness of social identities and the ways in which they shape experiences of oppression and privilege. In imaginary societies, understanding the intersectionality of identities—such as race, gender, and sexual orientation—allows activists to address the unique challenges faced by individuals at these intersections. This perspective is crucial in examining the impact of LGBTQ movements, as these movements often intersect with broader struggles for racial and economic justice.

Identity Politics focuses on the political interests and perspectives of specific social groups. Activism rooted in identity politics seeks to empower marginalized communities by affirming their identities and advocating for their rights. In imaginary societies, identity politics can mobilize individuals around shared experiences and foster solidarity among diverse groups.

Transformative Change

The impact of activism on imaginary societies can be observed through transformative changes in social norms, policies, and cultural representations. Activism challenges hegemonic narratives and opens up spaces for alternative voices and perspectives.

Social Norms Activism can lead to significant shifts in social norms, as seen in the LGBTQ movements across various imaginary societies. For instance, in the dystopian society of Xylon, the LGBTQ community's activism challenged deeply entrenched beliefs about gender and sexuality. Through protests, advocacy campaigns, and grassroots organizing, activists in Xylon were able to shift public perceptions, ultimately leading to greater acceptance and visibility of LGBTQ individuals.

Policy Changes Activism often results in concrete policy changes that enhance the rights and protections of marginalized groups. In Zephyria, a utopian society that values equality and social justice, the LGBTQ movement successfully lobbied for comprehensive anti-discrimination legislation. This legal framework not only protected LGBTQ individuals from discrimination in employment and housing but also served as a model for other societies grappling with similar issues.

Cultural Representations The impact of activism extends to cultural representations, as activists work to challenge stereotypes and promote diverse narratives. In Apolonia, a post-apocalyptic society, LGBTQ activists utilized art and storytelling to reclaim their narratives and highlight the resilience of their community. By creating spaces for LGBTQ voices in literature, film, and visual arts, activists in Apolonia fostered a sense of belonging and visibility for marginalized identities.

Challenges and Resistance

Despite the transformative potential of activism, it is essential to acknowledge the challenges and resistance that activists face in imaginary societies.

Systemic Oppression Activists often confront systemic oppression that seeks to maintain the status quo. In Xylon, LGBTQ activists faced violent backlash and repression from state authorities, highlighting the dangers of challenging entrenched power structures. This resistance can manifest in various forms, including legal barriers, social stigmatization, and even physical violence.

Internal Divisions Within activist movements, internal divisions can also hinder progress. In Zephyria, while the LGBTQ community celebrated diversity, tensions arose between different factions advocating for varying approaches to activism. These divisions can weaken collective efforts and create fragmentation within movements, ultimately impacting their effectiveness.

Fatigue and Burnout Activism can lead to emotional fatigue and burnout among activists, particularly in the face of persistent challenges. In Apolonia, where the struggle for LGBTQ rights was compounded by the societal collapse, activists faced the dual burden of rebuilding their communities while advocating for their rights. This exhaustion can limit the sustainability of activist efforts and hinder long-term change.

Conclusion

The impact of activism on imaginary societies is profound and multifaceted. Through the lens of social movement theory, intersectionality, and identity politics, we can understand how activism shapes social norms, influences policy changes, and transforms cultural representations. However, activists must navigate significant challenges and resistance, which can complicate their efforts for change. Ultimately, the resilience and creativity of activists in imaginary societies exemplify the enduring power of collective action in the pursuit of justice and equality.

The Intersectionality of Identity and Activism in Imaginary Societies

The concept of intersectionality, first coined by legal scholar Kimberlé Crenshaw, provides a vital framework for understanding how various aspects of identity—such as race, gender, sexuality, class, and ability—interact to shape individual experiences and social dynamics. In the context of imaginary societies, intersectionality serves as a lens through which we can analyze the multifaceted nature of identity and activism, revealing the complex interplay between diverse social categories and the movements that arise to advocate for rights and recognition.

Defining Intersectionality

Intersectionality posits that individuals do not experience oppression or privilege in isolation; rather, they navigate a web of interconnected identities that influence their social positioning and lived realities. The equation that often represents this concept can be expressed as:

$$O = f(I_1, I_2, I_3, \ldots, I_n)$$

where O represents the overall experience of oppression or privilege, and $I_1, I_2, I_3, \ldots, I_n$ denote the various intersecting identities (e.g., race, gender, sexuality). This function illustrates that the impact of any single identity cannot be fully understood without considering its interaction with others.

The Role of Intersectionality in Activism

In imaginary societies, activism often emerges as a response to the unique challenges faced by individuals at the intersection of multiple identities. For instance, in the dystopian society of Xylon, LGBTQ activists may confront not only homophobia but also systemic racism and economic inequality. The activism in such contexts is not monolithic; it is shaped by the diverse experiences of its members. This complexity necessitates a more nuanced approach to advocacy, as seen in the following examples:

- **Xylon:** The LGBTQ movements in Xylon have had to address issues of racial discrimination within their own community. Key figures such as activist Zara N'Kosi have highlighted the need for inclusivity, advocating for the recognition of queer people of color who often face compounded discrimination. Their activism emphasizes the importance of creating spaces where all identities are acknowledged and valued.

- **Zephyria:** In the utopian society of Zephyria, the celebration of diversity is central to its identity. However, even in this seemingly ideal society, intersectionality reveals challenges. LGBTQ individuals from lower socioeconomic backgrounds may still experience exclusion despite the overarching ideals of equality. Activists in Zephyria have organized workshops and community events that focus specifically on the intersection of class and sexuality, fostering dialogues that bridge these divides.

- **Apolonia:** The post-apocalyptic society of Apolonia presents a different scenario where survival takes precedence over identity politics. However, the LGBTQ community has developed support networks that recognize the intersectionality of their identities. Activists emphasize the importance of solidarity among marginalized groups, as they collectively navigate the harsh realities of their new world. The formation of alliances with other oppressed communities has proven essential for survival and advocacy.

Challenges of Intersectionality in Activism

While intersectionality provides a vital framework for understanding identity and activism, it also presents challenges. Activists may struggle with the following issues:

1. **Fragmentation of Movements:** In some cases, the focus on specific identities can lead to fragmentation within movements. For instance, in Xylon, the LGBTQ community may find itself divided along racial lines, with different groups prioritizing distinct issues. This fragmentation can weaken collective efforts and dilute the impact of activism.

2. **Resource Allocation:** Activists often face difficulties in addressing the needs of individuals at the intersection of multiple identities due to limited resources. In Zephyria, while the society promotes equality, funding for initiatives that specifically target intersectional issues may be scarce, leading to the marginalization of certain voices within the LGBTQ community.

3. **Resistance to Intersectional Approaches:** There can be resistance from within movements to fully embrace intersectionality. Some activists may prioritize a singular identity (e.g., sexual orientation) over others, believing that addressing one issue at a time is more effective. This resistance can hinder the development of comprehensive strategies that address the complexities of identity.

Conclusion

The intersectionality of identity and activism in imaginary societies underscores the importance of recognizing and addressing the diverse experiences of individuals within these contexts. By embracing a holistic understanding of identity, activists can cultivate more inclusive movements that honor the multiplicity of experiences and foster solidarity across various social categories. As we explore the case studies of Xylon, Zephyria, and Apolonia, it becomes clear that the intersectional approach is not merely an academic concept but a practical necessity for effective activism in the face of complex social realities. This understanding will be pivotal as we delve deeper into the specific movements and their impacts in the subsequent chapters of this book.

Key Themes and Concepts Explored in the Case Studies

In this section, we delve into the key themes and concepts that emerge from the case studies of LGBTQ movements across the imaginary societies of Xylon, Zephyria, and Apolonia. These themes not only highlight the unique challenges faced by LGBTQ communities but also underscore the universal struggles for identity, acceptance, and activism that resonate across different societal contexts.

Intersectionality and Identity

A central theme in the case studies is the concept of intersectionality, which refers to the interconnected nature of social categorizations such as race, class, gender, and sexual orientation. This concept, originally coined by Kimberlé Crenshaw, is crucial in understanding how various forms of discrimination overlap and compound the experiences of individuals within the LGBTQ community. For instance, in Xylon, LGBTQ individuals from marginalized racial backgrounds face a dual burden of oppression, complicating their fight for rights and recognition. The case study highlights the necessity of an intersectional approach to activism, as it allows for a more nuanced understanding of the unique struggles faced by individuals at the intersections of multiple identities.

Activism as a Tool for Change

The role of activism is another significant theme that permeates the case studies. Activism is portrayed not merely as a response to oppression but as a proactive tool for social change. In Zephyria, the LGBTQ movements exemplify how organized efforts can lead to substantial societal shifts, including the establishment of inclusive policies and the celebration of diversity. The case studies illustrate various forms of activism, from grassroots movements to institutional advocacy, demonstrating the effectiveness of collective action in challenging systemic inequalities.

Cultural Representation and Visibility

Cultural representation and visibility are critical concepts explored in the context of LGBTQ movements across the societies. The case studies reveal how representation in media, politics, and culture can significantly influence public perception and acceptance of LGBTQ individuals. For example, in Zephyria, the portrayal of LGBTQ characters in popular media has led to increased acceptance and normalization of diverse identities. Conversely, in Xylon, the lack of representation has perpetuated stereotypes and discrimination, illustrating the power of visibility in shaping societal attitudes.

Resilience and Community Building

The theme of resilience emerges prominently in the case studies, particularly in the context of the LGBTQ movements in Apolonia. Following the collapse of societal structures, LGBTQ individuals have demonstrated remarkable resilience in the face of adversity. The establishment of support networks and community resources showcases the importance of solidarity and collective identity in overcoming challenges. The case studies highlight how community-building efforts not only provide immediate support but also foster a sense of belonging and empowerment among LGBTQ individuals.

The Role of Technology in Activism

The influence of technology on activism is another key theme that is explored. In the contemporary context of Xylon, digital platforms have become essential tools for organizing and mobilizing LGBTQ movements. Social media, in particular, has facilitated the dissemination of information and the creation of virtual communities, allowing marginalized voices to be heard. The case studies examine how technology can both empower activists and pose challenges, such as online harassment and misinformation, illustrating the complex relationship between technology and activism.

The Impact of Policy and Legislation

Finally, the impact of policy and legislation on LGBTQ rights is a recurring theme throughout the case studies. The examination of legal frameworks in each society reveals how laws can either uphold or undermine the rights of LGBTQ individuals. In Zephyria, progressive legislation has contributed to a more inclusive society, while in Xylon, oppressive laws have perpetuated discrimination.

The case studies underscore the importance of legal advocacy in the fight for equality, highlighting the need for ongoing efforts to challenge unjust policies.

Conclusion

In conclusion, the key themes and concepts explored in the case studies of LGBTQ movements across Xylon, Zephyria, and Apolonia provide valuable insights into the complexities of identity and activism in imaginary societies. By examining intersectionality, the role of activism, cultural representation, resilience, technology, and policy impact, we gain a deeper understanding of the multifaceted nature of the struggles faced by LGBTQ communities. These themes not only inform our understanding of the past but also offer lessons for future activism and advocacy in our own societies.

Chapter One: The Dystopian Society of Xylon

The Historical Origins of Xylon

Origin Story and Creation of Xylon

The origin story of Xylon is steeped in myth and historical narrative, reflecting the complex interplay of identity, culture, and power dynamics that characterize its society. According to the foundational myths of Xylon, the society was birthed from the ashes of a great cataclysm, a metaphorical and literal rebirth that established its unique social fabric. The cataclysm, often referred to as the "Great Sundering," was a devastating event that not only reshaped the physical landscape but also redefined the social and political structures of the remnants of civilization.

The Great Sundering

The Great Sundering was marked by a series of natural disasters, wars, and societal upheavals that fragmented existing communities. This fragmentation is theorized to have led to a new understanding of identity, as individuals were forced to navigate their existence in a world where traditional structures no longer provided support or safety. As a result, the survivors of the Sundering began to form new alliances based on shared experiences of trauma and resilience, leading to the early formation of what would become Xylon.

Philosophical Foundations

The philosophical underpinnings of Xylon can be traced back to the teachings of early leaders known as the "Founders." These individuals emphasized the importance of collective identity and the necessity of activism as a means of survival. Their teachings are encapsulated in the tenet:

$$\text{Identity} + \text{Activism} = \text{Survival} \qquad (1)$$

This equation illustrates the belief that a shared identity among the survivors, coupled with active engagement in societal restructuring, was essential for the formation of a cohesive society. The Founders posited that identity could not be static; rather, it must evolve in response to the challenges posed by the new world.

Social and Political Structures

As Xylon emerged from the chaos, its social and political structures began to take shape. The society was organized around a council system, where representatives from various factions—each representing different identities and experiences—came together to make decisions. This system was revolutionary in its inclusivity, allowing for a multitude of voices to be heard, albeit not without its challenges. The council's formation was rooted in the belief that power should be decentralized to prevent the rise of oppressive hierarchies that had characterized pre-Sundering societies.

However, the ideal of inclusivity often clashed with the realities of governance. Tensions arose as different factions vied for influence, leading to internal conflicts that threatened the fragile unity of Xylon. These conflicts often revolved around differing interpretations of identity and the role of activism within the society. For instance, the LGBTQ community in Xylon faced unique challenges as they sought representation within the council. Their struggle highlighted the complexities of intersectionality, as they navigated both their sexual identity and the overarching identity of Xylon as a whole.

Cultural Narratives and Identity Formation

Cultural narratives played a pivotal role in shaping the identity of Xylon. Storytelling became a vital tool for the community, allowing individuals to share their experiences and forge connections across different identities. The oral tradition of recounting the tales of the Founders and the events of the Great Sundering fostered a sense of belonging and collective memory among the inhabitants of Xylon.

One prominent narrative that emerged was that of the "Resilient Ones," a term used to describe those who not only survived the Sundering but thrived in its aftermath. This narrative served to empower marginalized groups, including the

LGBTQ community, by framing their struggles as integral to the larger story of Xylon's creation.

Conclusion

In conclusion, the origin story and creation of Xylon is a testament to the resilience of its people and the complexities of identity formation in the wake of catastrophe. The interplay between activism and identity has been central to the society's evolution, shaping its social and political structures and fostering a culture of inclusivity. The challenges faced by various communities, particularly the LGBTQ movement, underscore the ongoing struggle for representation and recognition within Xylon. As the society continues to evolve, the lessons learned from its origin story remain relevant, reminding its inhabitants of the power of collective identity and the necessity of activism in forging a just and equitable society.

Evolution of Xylon's Social and Political Structures

The evolution of Xylon's social and political structures is a complex narrative intertwined with the identity and activism of its inhabitants. To understand this evolution, we must first explore the foundational elements that shaped Xylon's society. The society of Xylon emerged from a tumultuous historical context, characterized by conflict, oppression, and the struggle for recognition and rights.

Foundational Elements

At its inception, Xylon was founded on principles that initially promised equality and justice. However, as the society developed, these ideals were often overshadowed by authoritarian governance and systemic discrimination. The political structure of Xylon can be described through the lens of multiple theoretical frameworks, including Foucault's theory of power and Gramsci's concept of hegemony.

$$P = \frac{F}{R} \qquad (2)$$

Where P represents power, F symbolizes the force exerted by the ruling class, and R denotes the resistance from the marginalized groups. In Xylon, the ruling elite utilized various mechanisms of control to maintain their dominance, leading to a society marked by oppression and inequality.

Social Stratification

As Xylon's society evolved, social stratification became increasingly pronounced. The classification of individuals based on identity—such as gender, sexuality, and class—created distinct social hierarchies. The LGBTQ community, in particular, faced systemic marginalization, which was reinforced by both cultural norms and institutional policies. The intersectionality of these identities compounded the struggles faced by individuals within the LGBTQ community.

$$S = I + C + E \qquad (3)$$

Where S represents social stratification, I is the identity of individuals, C is the cultural context, and E denotes economic factors. This equation illustrates how various elements contribute to the overall structure of society in Xylon, leading to the exclusion of certain groups from political and social participation.

Political Evolution

The political landscape of Xylon has undergone significant transformations, particularly in response to activism and resistance movements. Initially, the governance of Xylon was characterized by a centralized authority that suppressed dissent. However, as activism gained momentum, particularly from the LGBTQ community, a shift began to occur.

Activists employed various strategies to challenge the status quo, including protests, advocacy campaigns, and grassroots organizing. Notable figures emerged during this period, such as *Ayla Korr*, a prominent LGBTQ activist who played a crucial role in mobilizing support for equal rights. The activism of Korr and others led to the establishment of organizations aimed at promoting LGBTQ rights and challenging oppressive policies.

Institutional Responses

In response to mounting pressure from activists, the political structures of Xylon began to adapt. Reforms were introduced, albeit slowly and often grudgingly. The government established the *Xylon Equality Commission* (XEC) to address issues of discrimination and promote inclusivity. However, the effectiveness of the XEC was often hampered by bureaucratic inertia and resistance from conservative factions within the government.

Despite these challenges, the LGBTQ community in Xylon demonstrated remarkable resilience. Activists continued to push for change, leveraging social media and digital platforms to amplify their voices and connect with allies both within and outside Xylon. This digital activism became a powerful tool for mobilization, allowing for the rapid dissemination of information and the organization of protests.

Contemporary Issues

Today, the social and political structures of Xylon are marked by ongoing tensions between progressive movements and conservative elements. While significant strides have been made in terms of legal recognition and rights for the LGBTQ community, challenges persist. Issues such as discrimination in employment, healthcare access, and societal stigma continue to affect the lives of many individuals.

The evolution of Xylon's social and political structures serves as a testament to the power of activism and the importance of identity in shaping societal norms. As activists continue to advocate for change, the legacy of resistance and resilience remains a central theme in Xylon's ongoing narrative.

In conclusion, the evolution of Xylon's social and political structures reflects a dynamic interplay between power, identity, and activism. Understanding this evolution is crucial for comprehending the broader implications of LGBTQ movements and their impact on imaginary societies. As we delve deeper into the case studies of Xylon, we will uncover the intricate ways in which these themes manifest and influence the lives of individuals within this unique society.

Key Events and Movements in Xylon's History

The history of Xylon is marked by significant events and movements that have shaped its social and political landscape. Understanding these key moments is essential to grasping the evolution of identity and activism within this dystopian society.

The Rise of the Oppressive Regime

The oppressive regime in Xylon emerged following a catastrophic civil war that left the nation in disarray. The war, fueled by socio-economic disparities and ethnic tensions, culminated in the establishment of a totalitarian government that prioritized control over individual freedoms. This regime utilized propaganda and surveillance to stifle dissent, leading to the systematic oppression of marginalized communities, including the LGBTQ population.

The Formation of the First LGBTQ Rights Organization

In the wake of the regime's establishment, the first LGBTQ rights organization, *Xylon United*, was formed in 2035. This grassroots movement sought to provide a safe space for LGBTQ individuals and advocate for their rights. The organization's founders, a diverse group of activists including the charismatic leader Zara Kade, utilized underground meetings and covert pamphleteering to mobilize support. This marked the beginning of organized resistance against the oppressive regime.

The Great Protest of 2042

One of the most pivotal events in Xylon's history was the Great Protest of 2042. Triggered by the government's brutal crackdown on a peaceful LGBTQ pride parade, thousands of citizens took to the streets in solidarity. This protest not only highlighted the struggles of the LGBTQ community but also ignited a broader movement for civil rights across various marginalized groups. The protest culminated in a violent confrontation with state forces, resulting in numerous injuries and arrests. Despite the harsh repercussions, the event galvanized the population and drew international attention to the plight of Xylon's citizens.

The Formation of the Coalition for Equality

In 2045, in response to the growing unrest, a coalition of various activist groups, including labor unions, women's rights organizations, and LGBTQ advocates, formed the *Coalition for Equality*. This coalition aimed to unify the disparate movements within Xylon and present a united front against the oppressive regime. The Coalition's platform emphasized intersectionality, recognizing that the struggles of LGBTQ individuals were intrinsically linked to those of other marginalized communities. This collaboration led to increased visibility and support for LGBTQ rights within the broader social justice movement.

The Rebellion of 2049

The Rebellion of 2049 marked a significant turning point in Xylon's history. After years of oppression, a series of coordinated uprisings broke out across the nation, led by the Coalition for Equality. The rebellion was characterized by its diverse participation, with LGBTQ activists playing a crucial role in organizing protests, disseminating information, and providing support to those in need. The movement's slogan, "Freedom for All, Not Just Some!", resonated deeply with the populace, reflecting the collective desire for a more inclusive society.

The Declaration of Rights in 2051

In the aftermath of the Rebellion, the government was forced to negotiate with the Coalition for Equality, leading to the historic Declaration of Rights in 2051. This document recognized the fundamental rights of all citizens, including the rights of LGBTQ individuals. While the declaration was a monumental achievement, it was met with resistance from conservative factions within the government, leading to ongoing tensions and challenges in its implementation.

The Ongoing Struggle for Acceptance

Despite the progress made, the LGBTQ community in Xylon continues to face challenges. Discrimination and violence against LGBTQ individuals remain prevalent, and activists are constantly working to ensure that the rights outlined in the Declaration are upheld. The ongoing struggle for acceptance is exemplified by the annual *Pride in Resistance* events, which celebrate LGBTQ identity while simultaneously advocating for continued activism and awareness.

Theoretical Framework

To analyze these events, it is essential to apply a theoretical framework that encompasses the concepts of identity, oppression, and activism. The intersectionality theory, proposed by Kimberlé Crenshaw, serves as a vital lens through which to understand the complexities of identity in Xylon. By recognizing that individuals possess multiple, overlapping identities, we can better comprehend how these identities interact with systems of oppression and influence activism.

Conclusion

The key events and movements in Xylon's history illustrate the resilience and determination of its citizens, particularly the LGBTQ community, in the face of oppression. From the formation of early organizations to the significant protests and rebellions, these moments have shaped the identity and activism landscape in Xylon. As the struggle for rights and acceptance continues, the lessons learned from these historical events remain crucial for future generations of activists.

The Relationship Between Identity and Oppression in Xylon

In the dystopian society of Xylon, the relationship between identity and oppression is a complex and multifaceted phenomenon. This section explores how various identities are constructed, perceived, and ultimately oppressed within the societal framework of Xylon. Through the lens of critical theory, particularly intersectionality and social constructivism, we can better understand the dynamics at play.

Theoretical Framework

Intersectionality, a term coined by Kimberlé Crenshaw, posits that individuals experience oppression in varying configurations and degrees based on their intersecting identities, such as race, gender, sexuality, and class. In Xylon, the intersection of these identities creates unique experiences of marginalization. For instance, LGBTQ individuals in Xylon do not merely face oppression due to their sexual orientation but also contend with additional layers of discrimination based on their race or socio-economic status.

Social constructivism further elucidates how identities are not inherent or fixed but are shaped by societal norms and values. In Xylon, the dominant narrative constructs certain identities as inferior or deviant, leading to systemic oppression. This construction of identity is reflected in laws, cultural practices, and societal expectations that dictate what is deemed acceptable.

Identity Categories and Their Implications

In Xylon, identities are categorized into rigid binaries that reinforce oppressive structures. For example, the government enforces strict gender norms, which marginalize those who identify outside the traditional male-female dichotomy. The LGBTQ community faces significant challenges as their identities are often criminalized, leading to widespread discrimination and violence.

$$O = f(I, S) \qquad (4)$$

Where O represents oppression, I represents identity, and S represents societal norms. This equation suggests that the level of oppression experienced by individuals in Xylon is a function of their identity and the prevailing societal norms.

Case Studies of Oppression

The Criminalization of LGBTQ Identities In Xylon, LGBTQ identities are not only marginalized but also criminalized. Laws exist that specifically target same-sex relationships, leading to arrests and imprisonment. For instance, the case of "The Xylon Five," a group of LGBTQ activists who were arrested for organizing a pride march, highlights the oppressive legal framework that seeks to silence dissent and erase non-conforming identities. Their subsequent trial was a public spectacle designed to reinforce the state's narrative that LGBTQ identities are aberrant.

Cultural Oppression Culturally, Xylon perpetuates stereotypes that further entrench oppression. Media representations of LGBTQ individuals often depict them as villains or tragic figures, which normalizes discrimination and fosters a culture of fear. The portrayal of LGBTQ characters in Xylon's popular television shows and films serves to reinforce societal prejudices, making it difficult for individuals to express their true identities without fear of backlash.

Resistance and Resilience

Despite the oppressive environment, the LGBTQ community in Xylon has demonstrated remarkable resilience. Activists employ various strategies to combat oppression, including underground networks that provide support and resources. For example, the "Rainbow Coalition," a grassroots organization, has emerged as a beacon of hope, offering safe spaces for LGBTQ individuals to gather and share their experiences. Their motto, "We are here, we are valid," serves as a powerful counter-narrative to the dominant discourse that seeks to erase their identities.

Moreover, the community has utilized art and performance as forms of resistance. The annual "Xylon Pride Festival," though illegal, has become a symbol of defiance against the oppressive regime. Participants risk their safety to celebrate their identities and demand recognition, showcasing the indomitable spirit of the LGBTQ community in Xylon.

Conclusion

The relationship between identity and oppression in Xylon is characterized by a complex interplay of societal norms, legal frameworks, and cultural representations. The oppressive structures that marginalize LGBTQ identities are deeply entrenched, yet the resilience and activism of the community serve as a testament to the power of identity in the face of adversity. Understanding this relationship is crucial for recognizing the ongoing struggles within Xylon and the need for continued advocacy for LGBTQ rights.

In summary, the exploration of identity and oppression in Xylon reveals the necessity of intersectional approaches to activism. By acknowledging the diverse experiences within the LGBTQ community, advocates can better address the multifaceted nature of oppression and work towards a more inclusive society.

The LGBTQ Movements on Xylon

Key Figures and Organizations in LGBTQ Activism on Xylon

In the dystopian society of Xylon, LGBTQ activism has emerged as a vital force for change, challenging oppressive structures and advocating for the rights of marginalized communities. This section explores the key figures and organizations that have played significant roles in the LGBTQ movements on Xylon, examining their contributions, struggles, and the theoretical frameworks that underpin their activism.

Key Figures in LGBTQ Activism

The LGBTQ movement in Xylon has been shaped by a diverse array of activists who have dedicated their lives to the fight for equality and recognition. Among them, three prominent figures stand out:

- **Ayla Kahn:** A prominent transgender activist, Ayla has been at the forefront of advocating for transgender rights in Xylon. Her work focuses on raising awareness about the unique challenges faced by transgender individuals, including access to healthcare, legal recognition, and protection from violence. Ayla's activism is grounded in the theory of *intersectionality*, which emphasizes the interconnected nature of social categorizations such as race, gender, and sexual orientation. By highlighting how these identities overlap, Ayla seeks to address the compounded discrimination faced by marginalized groups within the LGBTQ community.

- **Jasper Lin:** A gay rights activist and founder of the organization *Unity for Change*, Jasper has been instrumental in mobilizing grassroots efforts to combat discrimination against LGBTQ individuals in Xylon. His approach combines elements of *critical theory*, which critiques societal structures of power and oppression, with practical strategies for community organizing. Jasper's campaigns have focused on advocating for anti-discrimination laws and promoting LGBTQ representation in political offices.

- **Rhea Patel:** As a bisexual activist and artist, Rhea uses her creative talents to challenge societal norms and promote visibility for bisexual individuals in

Xylon. Through her art, she addresses the misconceptions and stereotypes that often plague the bisexual community. Rhea's work is informed by *queer theory*, which questions the binary understanding of gender and sexuality, and seeks to create space for fluid identities within the LGBTQ spectrum.

Key Organizations in LGBTQ Activism

In addition to individual activists, several organizations have emerged as pivotal players in the LGBTQ movement on Xylon. These organizations provide resources, support, and advocacy for LGBTQ individuals, fostering community and resilience in the face of adversity.

- **Xylon Pride Coalition (XPC):** Founded in the wake of a violent crackdown on LGBTQ gatherings, the Xylon Pride Coalition has become a leading organization in the fight for LGBTQ rights. XPC organizes annual pride events, educational workshops, and advocacy campaigns aimed at raising awareness about LGBTQ issues. Their work is rooted in the principles of *social justice*, emphasizing the importance of equity and inclusion for all members of society.

- **Safe Haven Network (SHN):** This organization focuses on providing safe spaces and support for LGBTQ youth who have been displaced or rejected by their families. SHN offers counseling, housing assistance, and educational programs to empower young LGBTQ individuals. Their approach is informed by the theory of *trauma-informed care*, recognizing the profound impact of trauma on mental health and well-being, and emphasizing the need for supportive environments.

- **Trans Rights Advocacy Group (TRAG):** TRAG is dedicated to advocating for the rights of transgender individuals in Xylon. The organization works to educate the public about transgender issues, provides legal assistance for name and gender marker changes, and campaigns for comprehensive healthcare access. Their activism is guided by the principles of *human rights*, asserting that all individuals deserve to live authentically and without fear of discrimination or violence.

Challenges Faced by Activists and Organizations

Despite the progress made by LGBTQ activists and organizations in Xylon, numerous challenges persist. Activists often face backlash from conservative factions within society, leading to threats, violence, and legal repercussions. Moreover, internal divisions within the LGBTQ community can hinder collective action, as differing priorities and experiences create tensions among various identity groups.

The theoretical framework of *postcolonial theory* can be applied to understand these dynamics, as it examines the lingering effects of colonialism on identity and power structures. In Xylon, the legacy of oppressive regimes has shaped societal attitudes toward LGBTQ individuals, complicating the struggle for acceptance and equality.

Conclusion

The key figures and organizations in LGBTQ activism on Xylon illustrate the resilience and determination of the community in the face of adversity. Through their efforts, they challenge oppressive systems, advocate for marginalized voices, and strive for a more inclusive society. As the movement continues to evolve, it remains essential to recognize the diverse identities and experiences within the LGBTQ community, ensuring that all voices are heard and valued in the ongoing fight for justice and equality.

Struggles and Achievements of the LGBTQ Movements on Xylon

The LGBTQ movements on Xylon have traversed a tumultuous landscape characterized by both significant struggles and remarkable achievements. The societal structure of Xylon, steeped in historical oppression and rigid norms, has posed numerous challenges for the LGBTQ community. However, these adversities have also catalyzed activism that has led to meaningful change and progress.

Theoretical Framework

To understand the struggles and achievements of the LGBTQ movements on Xylon, we can apply Judith Butler's theory of gender performativity, which posits that gender is not a fixed identity but rather a series of acts and performances that individuals engage in. This theoretical lens helps to illuminate how the rigid gender norms in Xylon have been both enforced and resisted through activism. Moreover, intersectionality, as articulated by Kimberlé Crenshaw, is crucial for analyzing the varied experiences within the LGBTQ community, particularly how race, class, and gender identity intersect to create unique struggles.

Struggles Faced by the LGBTQ Community

The LGBTQ community in Xylon has encountered systemic discrimination that has manifested in various forms:

- **Legal Barriers:** Historically, Xylon's legal framework has criminalized same-sex relationships and gender non-conformity. Laws that enforced heteronormativity not only marginalized LGBTQ individuals but also perpetuated violence against them. Activists have often found themselves in direct conflict with the state, advocating for the repeal of these oppressive laws.

- **Social Stigma:** The deeply ingrained societal norms in Xylon have fostered an environment of stigma and discrimination. LGBTQ individuals have faced ostracization from their families and communities, leading to mental health crises and, in severe cases, homelessness. The social stigma surrounding LGBTQ identities has often deterred individuals from openly expressing their true selves, which in turn stifles community growth and solidarity.

- **Violence and Harassment:** The LGBTQ community in Xylon has been subjected to various forms of violence, including hate crimes and state-sanctioned violence. Activists have organized to raise awareness of these issues, often at great personal risk. The intersection of race and sexual orientation further complicates these struggles, as individuals from marginalized racial backgrounds face compounded discrimination.

- **Internal Divisions:** The LGBTQ community on Xylon is not monolithic; it encompasses a diverse range of identities and experiences. Internal divisions based on race, socioeconomic status, and gender identity have sometimes hindered collective action. For example, queer individuals of color have often felt sidelined in predominantly white LGBTQ movements, leading to the formation of separate organizations that address their unique challenges.

Achievements of the LGBTQ Movements

Despite these struggles, the LGBTQ movements on Xylon have achieved significant milestones that have transformed the societal landscape:

- **Legal Reforms:** Activism has led to the introduction of legal protections for LGBTQ individuals. Landmark cases in the Xylonian courts have resulted in the decriminalization of same-sex relationships and the recognition of LGBTQ rights. These legal victories have not only provided a framework for protection but have also empowered individuals to advocate for their rights.

- **Visibility and Representation:** The rise of LGBTQ visibility in Xylon has been a crucial achievement. Activists have utilized various platforms, including social media and public demonstrations, to raise awareness about LGBTQ issues. The annual Pride Parade, which began as a small gathering, has grown into a significant event that draws thousands of participants and allies, showcasing the community's diversity and resilience.

- **Support Networks:** The establishment of support networks and organizations has been vital in providing resources for LGBTQ individuals. These organizations offer counseling, legal assistance, and safe spaces for community members. For instance, the "Xylon LGBTQ Alliance" has played a crucial role in connecting individuals with resources and fostering a sense of belonging.

- **Cultural Shifts:** The activism of the LGBTQ community has contributed to broader cultural shifts in Xylon. Increased representation in media and the arts has facilitated conversations about gender and sexuality, challenging traditional narratives. The success of LGBTQ artists and performers has not only validated diverse identities but has also inspired a new generation of activists.

Conclusion

The struggles and achievements of the LGBTQ movements on Xylon illustrate the complex interplay between identity and activism. While the community has faced significant challenges, the resilience and determination of its members have led to substantial progress. The ongoing fight for equality and recognition continues to inspire new generations of activists, ensuring that the legacy of struggle transforms into a future of hope and acceptance.

In summary, the LGBTQ movements on Xylon embody the essence of activism as a powerful force for change. By examining their journey, we gain insights into the broader implications of identity politics and the importance of solidarity in the face of adversity. The lessons learned from Xylon can serve as a beacon for other imaginary societies grappling with similar issues, highlighting the universal quest for dignity and recognition in the tapestry of human experience.

Challenges and Controversies Within the LGBTQ Community on Xylon

The LGBTQ community in Xylon faces a myriad of challenges and controversies that stem from both internal dynamics and external societal pressures. Understanding these issues requires a nuanced exploration of identity politics, intersectionality, and the socio-political landscape of Xylon.

Internal Divisions and Identity Politics

One of the most significant challenges within the LGBTQ community on Xylon is the fragmentation caused by differing identities and experiences. The intersectionality theory posits that individuals possess multiple identities that can shape their experiences of oppression and privilege (Crenshaw, 1989). In Xylon, this manifests in various factions within the LGBTQ community, each advocating for different priorities based on race, class, gender identity, and sexual orientation.

For instance, queer individuals of color often feel marginalized within the broader LGBTQ movement, which has historically centered around the experiences of white, cisgender gay men. This has led to the formation of subgroups that emphasize the need for inclusivity and representation, such as the Coalition for Intersectional LGBTQ Rights (CILR). The CILR argues for a more comprehensive approach that addresses the unique challenges faced by LGBTQ individuals from diverse backgrounds, advocating for policies that consider race and class alongside sexual orientation.

Controversies Over Representation

Representation is another contentious issue within the LGBTQ community on Xylon. The debate often centers around who gets to represent the community in activism and media. The concept of "tokenism" arises when individuals from marginalized groups are included in representation efforts merely to fulfill a quota, without genuine power or influence (Kumar, 2015).

For example, during the annual Pride festival in Xylon, the inclusion of a few queer people of color in promotional materials sparked outrage among activists who argued that the event's organizing committee failed to address systemic racism within the LGBTQ community. The backlash led to calls for a more equitable representation of all identities within the festival's planning and execution, emphasizing the need for authentic voices rather than symbolic gestures.

The Role of Social Media and Activism

Social media has become a double-edged sword for the LGBTQ community in Xylon. On one hand, platforms like XyloChat and InstaXylon provide spaces for activists to mobilize, share resources, and amplify marginalized voices. On the other hand, these platforms can also exacerbate divisions and spread misinformation.

The rise of "cancel culture" has led to public shaming of individuals within the community who are perceived as failing to meet certain ideological standards. This has created an environment of fear and self-censorship, where individuals may hesitate to voice their opinions for fear of backlash. A notable incident involved a prominent LGBTQ activist who was "canceled" after expressing concerns about the direction of the movement, leading to a heated debate about the boundaries of discourse and the importance of constructive criticism within activist spaces.

Conflict with Traditional Norms and Values

The LGBTQ community in Xylon also grapples with the tension between progressive values and traditional norms. Many LGBTQ individuals face familial and societal rejection, particularly from conservative factions that uphold heteronormative values. This conflict often leads to a phenomenon known as "identity concealment," where individuals feel compelled to hide their sexual orientation or gender identity to maintain familial or social acceptance (Meyer, 2003).

Furthermore, the backlash against LGBTQ rights in Xylon has intensified in recent years, with conservative groups advocating for "traditional family values" and opposing LGBTQ-inclusive policies. This has resulted in protests and counter-protests, often leading to confrontations that highlight the deep societal divisions regarding LGBTQ rights. The ongoing struggle for recognition and equality has prompted some activists to question the effectiveness of traditional forms of protest, leading to discussions about alternative strategies that prioritize dialogue and education over confrontation.

Conclusion

In conclusion, the challenges and controversies within the LGBTQ community on Xylon reflect broader societal dynamics and underscore the importance of intersectionality in activism. As the community continues to navigate these complexities, it becomes increasingly vital to foster inclusivity, representation, and open dialogue. Addressing these internal conflicts not only strengthens the movement but also enhances the potential for meaningful change in Xylon's socio-political landscape.

The Resilience and Unity of the LGBTQ Community on Xylon

The LGBTQ community on Xylon has demonstrated remarkable resilience and unity in the face of systemic oppression and societal challenges. This section explores the factors contributing to this resilience, the theoretical frameworks that underpin community solidarity, and specific examples that illustrate the strength of LGBTQ activism on Xylon.

Theoretical Frameworks of Resilience and Unity

Resilience, in the context of marginalized communities, can be understood through the lens of *community resilience theory*, which posits that communities can withstand and rebound from adversities through collective action and shared identity. [?] This theory emphasizes the importance of social networks, community engagement, and collective efficacy in fostering resilience.

Furthermore, *intersectionality*, a concept introduced by Kimberlé Crenshaw, provides a framework for understanding how overlapping identities—such as race, gender, and sexual orientation—affect the experiences of individuals within the LGBTQ community. [?] On Xylon, intersectionality has played a crucial role in fostering unity among diverse groups within the LGBTQ community, as individuals recognize their shared struggles while also acknowledging the unique challenges faced by different subgroups.

Challenges Faced by the LGBTQ Community on Xylon

Despite the community's resilience, LGBTQ individuals on Xylon have faced significant challenges, including:

- **Legal Discrimination:** Laws that criminalize same-sex relationships and deny basic rights to LGBTQ individuals have created a hostile environment, necessitating organized resistance.

- **Social Stigmatization:** Cultural narratives that promote heteronormativity have marginalized LGBTQ identities, leading to social ostracism and mental health issues.

- **Economic Disparities:** Many LGBTQ individuals experience economic hardships due to discrimination in the workplace, further complicating their ability to organize and advocate for rights.

These challenges have galvanized the LGBTQ community, fostering a sense of urgency and solidarity among its members.

Examples of Resilience and Unity

The resilience and unity of the LGBTQ community on Xylon can be illustrated through several key movements and events:

1. **The Pride March of Xylon:** An annual event that began as a small gathering in response to a violent crackdown on LGBTQ individuals in 2015. Over the years, it has grown into a massive celebration of identity and resistance, drawing participants from various backgrounds and fostering a sense of belonging. The march serves not only as a platform for visibility but also as a unifying force that strengthens community ties.

2. **The Coalition for LGBTQ Rights (CLR):** Formed in response to increasing legal discrimination, the CLR has become a central organization advocating for policy changes on Xylon. Through strategic alliances with other marginalized groups, the CLR exemplifies how intersectional activism can create a more robust front against oppression. Their campaigns have successfully lobbied for the repeal of discriminatory laws and the implementation of inclusive policies.

3. **Support Networks and Safe Spaces:** In the wake of societal stigma, grassroots initiatives have emerged to create safe spaces for LGBTQ individuals. Community centers, online forums, and support groups provide not only emotional support but also resources for advocacy and education. These networks have proven vital in fostering resilience, as they allow individuals to share their experiences and strategies for coping with adversity.

The Role of Activism in Fostering Unity

Activism has played a pivotal role in fostering unity within the LGBTQ community on Xylon. Through collective action, individuals have been able to confront injustices and advocate for their rights, leading to a stronger sense of identity and purpose.

$$U = f(A, R, C) \tag{5}$$

where U represents unity, A is the level of activism, R denotes resources available to the community, and C signifies the collective identity shared among members. This equation illustrates that unity is a function of active engagement, resource mobilization, and shared identity, all of which have been crucial in the LGBTQ movements on Xylon.

Conclusion

The resilience and unity of the LGBTQ community on Xylon are testaments to the power of collective action in the face of adversity. By leveraging theoretical frameworks such as community resilience and intersectionality, the community has navigated significant challenges and emerged stronger. Through events like the Pride March, the work of organizations like the CLR, and the establishment of support networks, the LGBTQ community on Xylon continues to inspire hope and foster solidarity, serving as a model for other marginalized groups facing similar struggles.

Chapter Two: The Utopian Society of Zephyria

The Founding Principles of Zephyria

Ideals of Equality and Social Justice in Zephyria

In Zephyria, the founding principles are deeply rooted in the ideals of equality and social justice, which serve as the bedrock of its societal structure. These ideals are not merely aspirational; they are actively embedded in the laws, cultural practices, and daily lives of Zephyrians. The commitment to equality manifests itself in various forms, including economic equity, gender parity, and the celebration of diversity across all identities.

Theoretical Framework

The theoretical underpinning of equality in Zephyria can be traced back to several philosophical traditions, notably those of John Rawls and his theory of justice as fairness. According to Rawls, a just society is one that ensures the greatest benefit to the least advantaged members. In mathematical terms, this can be expressed as:

$$\text{Maximin Principle:} \quad \max \min U_i \tag{6}$$

where U_i represents the utility of individual i. This principle is crucial in shaping Zephyria's policies, which prioritize the needs of marginalized groups, including the LGBTQ community.

Moreover, the ideals of equality are reinforced by the concept of intersectionality, introduced by Kimberlé Crenshaw. Intersectionality posits that individuals experience oppression in varying configurations and degrees of intensity based on their overlapping identities. In Zephyria, this concept is integral to understanding how different forms of discrimination—be it based on gender, sexual orientation, race, or class—interact and affect individuals' experiences.

Practical Applications

The ideals of equality and social justice in Zephyria are operationalized through several key mechanisms:

- **Legislative Framework:** Zephyria has enacted comprehensive anti-discrimination laws that protect individuals from bias based on sexual orientation, gender identity, race, and other characteristics. The Zephyrian Equality Act mandates equal treatment in employment, housing, and public services, ensuring that no individual is denied their rights due to their identity.

- **Economic Policies:** Economic equity is pursued through progressive taxation and wealth redistribution policies. The government invests in social programs aimed at uplifting the most disadvantaged groups, including targeted support for LGBTQ individuals who may face economic hardships due to discrimination.

- **Educational Initiatives:** Education in Zephyria emphasizes inclusivity and the importance of understanding diverse identities. Schools incorporate curricula that teach students about LGBTQ history, rights, and contributions, fostering a culture of respect and acceptance from a young age.

- **Community Engagement:** Grassroots organizations play a vital role in promoting social justice in Zephyria. These organizations work to empower marginalized communities, providing resources, advocacy, and support networks that are crucial for fostering resilience and unity among diverse groups.

Challenges to Equality and Social Justice

Despite its progressive ideals, Zephyria is not without challenges. Issues such as systemic bias, economic disparities, and cultural resistance to change persist. For instance, while laws exist to protect LGBTQ rights, enforcement can be inconsistent, and discrimination may still occur in subtle forms. Additionally, some segments of the population may resist the ideals of equality, leading to social tensions.

An example of this resistance can be seen in the backlash against certain educational initiatives aimed at promoting LGBTQ inclusivity. While many Zephyrians support these efforts, there are pockets of opposition that argue against the necessity of such programs, claiming they undermine traditional values. This highlights the ongoing struggle between progressive ideals and conservative viewpoints within the society.

Conclusion

In summary, the ideals of equality and social justice in Zephyria are foundational to its identity as a utopian society. Through a combination of legislative measures, economic policies, educational initiatives, and community engagement, Zephyria strives to create an inclusive environment where all individuals, regardless of their identity, can thrive. However, the challenges that remain serve as a reminder that the journey towards true equality is ongoing, requiring constant vigilance, activism, and commitment from all members of society.

The resilience of Zephyrian citizens, particularly those in the LGBTQ community, exemplifies the spirit of activism that is essential in confronting these challenges. As Zephyria continues to evolve, the interplay between its ideals and the lived experiences of its citizens will shape the future of this imaginary society, ensuring that the pursuit of equality and social justice remains at the forefront of its collective consciousness.

The Concept of Utopia in Zephyria

The notion of utopia is central to understanding the societal fabric of Zephyria. Derived from the Greek words "ou" (not) and "topos" (place), the term utopia suggests an idealized society that is often unattainable. In Zephyria, this concept is not merely theoretical; it is woven into the very essence of its identity and governance. This section will explore the philosophical underpinnings of utopian thought as it applies to Zephyria, the challenges it faces, and the manifestations of its ideals in everyday life.

Philosophical Foundations of Utopianism

Utopianism in Zephyria is heavily influenced by the works of philosophers such as Thomas More, who envisioned a perfect society characterized by communal living and equality. More's utopia serves as a blueprint for Zephyria, where the ideals of cooperation and social harmony are paramount. The Zephyrian model draws on the following key principles:

- **Collectivism:** The belief that the community's well-being supersedes individual interests. This is reflected in policies that promote shared resources and collective decision-making.

- **Equity:** Zephyria strives for social justice, ensuring that all citizens have equal access to opportunities and resources, regardless of their background.

- **Sustainability:** An emphasis on environmental stewardship and responsible resource management to ensure the longevity of their utopian society.

These principles are not without their critics. Detractors argue that the idealism of Zephyria leads to complacency and a lack of critical engagement with societal flaws. The challenge lies in balancing the lofty ideals of utopia with the practical realities of governance and human behavior.

Challenges to Utopian Ideals

Despite its noble aspirations, Zephyria faces several challenges that threaten the realization of its utopian vision. These challenges include:

- **Diversity of Identity:** The presence of various identities within Zephyria complicates the implementation of a singular utopian vision. While the society promotes acceptance, tensions can arise when cultural practices or beliefs clash with the dominant utopian narrative.

- **Resource Allocation:** As a society that values equality, Zephyria must navigate the complexities of resource distribution. Disparities can emerge, leading to discontent among marginalized groups who feel overlooked in favor of the majority.

- **Political Dissent:** While Zephyria promotes democratic ideals, the existence of dissenting voices challenges the notion of a harmonious society. The government must balance the need for stability with the rights of individuals to voice opposition.

Real-World Examples of Utopian Practices

In practice, Zephyria has implemented several initiatives that embody its utopian ideals. For instance, the establishment of community gardens serves as a microcosm of collectivism, where citizens collaborate to cultivate food sustainably.

These gardens not only provide nourishment but also foster community bonds and a sense of shared purpose.

Moreover, the Zephyrian education system emphasizes inclusivity and critical thinking, encouraging students to engage with diverse perspectives. This approach aims to cultivate a generation that is not only aware of utopian ideals but also equipped to challenge and refine them.

Conclusion: The Pursuit of Utopia in Zephyria

The concept of utopia in Zephyria is a dynamic interplay of ideals and realities. While the society strives for a perfect state characterized by equality and harmony, it must continuously confront the complexities of human identity and social dynamics. The ongoing pursuit of utopia requires a commitment to dialogue, adaptability, and an acknowledgment of the imperfections inherent in any society. As Zephyria navigates these challenges, it serves as a poignant reminder that the journey toward an ideal society is as significant as the destination itself.

$$U = \frac{E}{R} \cdot C \qquad (7)$$

In this equation, U represents the level of utopia achieved, E denotes the equity of resource distribution, R signifies the resistance to social change, and C reflects the collective commitment of the populace. This formula encapsulates the delicate balance that Zephyria must maintain in its quest for an ideal society.

The Role of Identity in Zephyria's Utopian Vision

In Zephyria, the concept of identity is intricately woven into the fabric of its utopian vision. This society, founded on principles of equality and social justice, places a significant emphasis on the recognition and celebration of diverse identities. The theoretical framework surrounding identity in Zephyria can be understood through several lenses, including social constructivism, intersectionality, and the role of collective memory.

Social Constructivism and Identity

Social constructivism posits that identities are not innate or fixed; rather, they are shaped by social interactions and cultural contexts. In Zephyria, this perspective allows for a fluid understanding of identity, where individuals are encouraged to define themselves based on their experiences and relationships. This approach fosters an environment where various identities—be they related to gender, sexuality, race, or ability—are acknowledged and valued.

$$I = f(S, C) \tag{8}$$

Where:

- I represents identity,
- S denotes social interactions,
- C symbolizes cultural contexts.

This equation illustrates that identity is a function of both social and cultural influences, reinforcing the idea that in Zephyria, identity is a dynamic construct.

Intersectionality in Identity Formation

The theory of intersectionality, coined by Kimberlé Crenshaw, plays a crucial role in understanding identity in Zephyria. It emphasizes that individuals experience multiple, overlapping identities that can lead to unique forms of discrimination or privilege. In Zephyria, the acknowledgment of intersectionality is fundamental to its utopian vision, as it seeks to dismantle hierarchies that often marginalize certain groups.

For example, the LGBTQ community in Zephyria is not monolithic; it encompasses a spectrum of identities, including but not limited to, transgender individuals, non-binary persons, and queer people of color. The intersection of these identities creates distinct experiences that must be recognized and addressed within the broader framework of social justice.

Collective Memory and Identity

Collective memory also plays a pivotal role in shaping identity within Zephyria. This concept refers to the shared pool of knowledge and information that a group of people collectively remembers. In Zephyria, collective memory is harnessed to foster a sense of belonging and community among its citizens. Historical narratives that celebrate diversity and resilience are integrated into the education system and public discourse, reinforcing the importance of identity in the societal fabric.

$$CM = \sum_{i=1}^{n} M_i \tag{9}$$

Where:

- CM represents collective memory,
- M_i denotes individual memories,
- n is the number of individuals in the community.

This equation indicates that collective memory is the sum of individual experiences, emphasizing that each person's identity contributes to the larger narrative of Zephyria.

Challenges and Critiques of Utopian Identity Politics

Despite the progressive ideals surrounding identity in Zephyria, challenges persist. Critics argue that the utopian vision can sometimes lead to superficial inclusivity, where the emphasis on diversity may overshadow the need for substantive change. For instance, while Zephyria celebrates LGBTQ identities, there may still be underlying systemic issues that perpetuate inequality, such as economic disparities or access to resources.

Furthermore, the ideal of a harmonious society can create pressure for individuals to conform to a singular narrative of identity, thus marginalizing those whose experiences do not fit neatly within the utopian framework. This tension raises important questions about the balance between collective identity and individual expression in Zephyria.

Conclusion

In conclusion, the role of identity in Zephyria's utopian vision is multifaceted and essential for fostering a society that values diversity and inclusivity. By embracing social constructivism, intersectionality, and collective memory, Zephyria aims to create a space where all identities are recognized and celebrated. However, it is crucial for the society to remain vigilant against the potential pitfalls of utopian ideals, ensuring that the pursuit of a perfect society does not come at the expense of individual experiences and struggles.

Challenges and Criticisms of Utopianism in Zephyria

Utopianism, while often celebrated for its ideals of equality and social justice, faces significant challenges and criticisms in the context of Zephyria. This section explores the theoretical underpinnings of utopian thought, the practical difficulties encountered in Zephyria, and the critiques that arise from its implementation.

Theoretical Foundations of Utopianism

Utopianism is grounded in the philosophical traditions of idealism and social constructivism, where the belief in a perfect society is often juxtaposed against the harsh realities of human nature and societal structures. The works of Thomas More, Karl Marx, and more contemporary theorists like Fredric Jameson provide a framework for understanding utopian aspirations. More's concept of a "utopia" as an ideal community challenges the status quo, while Marx's vision of a classless society critiques capitalist structures that perpetuate inequality. However, the idealism inherent in these visions often overlooks the complexities of human behavior, leading to potential disillusionment when applied in practice.

Practical Challenges in Zephyria

Despite its foundational principles, Zephyria grapples with several practical challenges that undermine its utopian vision.

- **Homogeneity vs. Diversity:** Zephyria's pursuit of equality has sometimes resulted in an enforced homogeneity, where individuality is suppressed in favor of a collective identity. This has led to tensions within the LGBTQ community, where diverse expressions of identity clash with the societal expectation of conformity. For instance, the Rainbow Alliance, a prominent LGBTQ organization in Zephyria, has faced criticism for prioritizing mainstream narratives of LGBTQ experience, thereby marginalizing voices from non-binary and queer communities.

- **Resource Allocation:** The ideal of equality in Zephyria has also been challenged by practical issues surrounding resource allocation. The emphasis on equal distribution has led to shortages in essential services, particularly in healthcare and education, which disproportionately affect marginalized groups, including LGBTQ individuals. The equation governing resource distribution can be expressed as:

$$R = \frac{E}{N}$$

where R is the resource per individual, E is the total resources available, and N is the population size. As the population increases without a corresponding increase in resources, the equality promised by Zephyria becomes increasingly difficult to maintain.

- **Resistance to Change:** The rigid adherence to utopian ideals has fostered resistance among those who feel excluded from the narrative. Activists advocating for more inclusive policies have faced backlash from traditionalists who view any deviation from the established norms as a threat to the societal fabric. This resistance can be encapsulated in the following dynamic:

$$C = \frac{I}{R}$$

where C represents the level of societal cohesion, I is the inclusivity of policies, and R is the resistance to change. A decrease in inclusivity leads to increased resistance, ultimately threatening the stability of the utopian vision.

Critiques of Utopian Ideals

Critics argue that the very nature of utopianism is flawed, as it often fails to account for the complexities of human existence. The philosopher Herbert Marcuse posits that utopian thought can become a form of escapism, detaching individuals from the pressing realities of social injustice. In Zephyria, this critique manifests in the form of disillusionment among citizens who feel that the utopian promise has not been fulfilled.

Furthermore, the idea of a "perfect society" implies a static state, which is inherently at odds with the dynamic nature of human relationships and societal evolution. The LGBTQ community in Zephyria has voiced concerns that the pursuit of a singular utopian ideal can overshadow the need for ongoing dialogue and adaptation to the changing social landscape. This is particularly evident in the backlash against the Zephyrian government's attempts to standardize LGBTQ rights, which, while well-intentioned, have often neglected the specific needs of diverse subgroups within the community.

Conclusion

In conclusion, while Zephyria's utopian vision offers an inspiring framework for equality and justice, it is not without its challenges and criticisms. The tension between idealism and practicality, the struggle for inclusivity, and the critiques of static utopian thought highlight the complexities of realizing a truly equitable society. As Zephyria continues to navigate these challenges, it must remain vigilant in addressing the diverse needs of its citizens, particularly those from the LGBTQ community, to avoid the pitfalls of a utopia that fails to live up to its promises.

The LGBTQ Movements on Zephyria

LGBTQ Rights and Acceptance in Zephyria

In the utopian society of Zephyria, the principles of equality and social justice are foundational to its identity. The societal framework is built upon the belief that all individuals, regardless of their sexual orientation or gender identity, deserve recognition, respect, and rights. This section explores the evolution of LGBTQ rights and acceptance in Zephyria, examining the theoretical underpinnings, societal challenges, and notable achievements within this community.

Theoretical Framework of LGBTQ Rights

The acceptance of LGBTQ individuals in Zephyria can be understood through the lens of several key theoretical frameworks, including *queer theory* and *intersectionality*. Queer theory challenges the binary understanding of gender and sexuality, promoting a fluid understanding of identity that aligns with Zephyria's foundational ideals. This theoretical approach emphasizes the importance of individual experiences and the rejection of normative constraints, allowing for a diverse representation of identities.

Intersectionality, as posited by Kimberlé Crenshaw, further enriches this understanding by highlighting how various forms of discrimination—such as those based on race, class, and gender—intersect with sexual orientation. In Zephyria, the acknowledgment of intersectionality has led to a more inclusive LGBTQ movement that addresses the unique challenges faced by individuals at these intersections.

Historical Context of LGBTQ Rights in Zephyria

Historically, Zephyria has embraced progressive values, which laid the groundwork for the acceptance of LGBTQ rights. The founding principles of Zephyria emphasized the importance of individual freedoms and the rejection of oppression in all forms. This was particularly relevant in the early days of Zephyria when the societal structure was being established. Influential movements, such as the *Rainbow Coalition*, emerged, advocating for the rights of LGBTQ individuals and pushing for legislative reforms that would ensure equality.

One pivotal moment in Zephyria's history was the *Equality Act* passed in 2050, which legally recognized LGBTQ rights and prohibited discrimination based on sexual orientation and gender identity. This legislation was a direct response to the advocacy efforts of various LGBTQ organizations, such as *Zephyr Pride* and *The Alliance for LGBTQ Rights*, which worked tirelessly to raise awareness and promote acceptance.

Current Status of LGBTQ Rights and Acceptance

As of the present day, LGBTQ rights in Zephyria are not only legally protected but are also widely accepted within the societal fabric. Public attitudes towards LGBTQ individuals are overwhelmingly positive, with extensive support from various sectors, including education, healthcare, and government. The Zephyrian government actively promotes LGBTQ rights through public campaigns, educational programs, and community outreach initiatives.

For example, the annual *Zephyr Pride Festival* serves as a celebration of diversity and inclusion, attracting thousands of participants from various backgrounds. This festival not only showcases the artistic and cultural contributions of LGBTQ individuals but also serves as a platform for advocacy, raising awareness about ongoing issues such as mental health, homelessness, and violence against LGBTQ individuals.

Challenges Faced by the LGBTQ Community

Despite the progressive stance on LGBTQ rights in Zephyria, challenges remain. While overt discrimination is rare, subtle forms of bias persist. For instance, LGBTQ youth may still experience bullying in schools, and there are ongoing discussions about the representation of LGBTQ individuals in media and politics. Additionally, the intersectional challenges faced by LGBTQ individuals of color highlight the need for continued advocacy and support.

The Zephyrian government has acknowledged these challenges and has implemented various initiatives to address them. Programs aimed at educating the public about LGBTQ issues and promoting inclusivity in schools have been established. Furthermore, mental health resources specifically designed for LGBTQ youth have been expanded, recognizing the unique pressures they face.

Conclusion

In conclusion, the journey towards LGBTQ rights and acceptance in Zephyria reflects a broader commitment to equality and social justice. Through a combination of legal protections, societal acceptance, and ongoing advocacy, Zephyria has created an environment where LGBTQ individuals can thrive. However, the work is not finished; continued vigilance and activism are essential to address the remaining challenges and ensure that Zephyria remains a beacon of hope and acceptance for all individuals, regardless of their identity.

$$\text{Acceptance Rate} = \frac{\text{Number of Supportive Individuals}}{\text{Total Population}} \times 100\% \quad (10)$$

This equation illustrates the importance of measuring societal acceptance quantitatively, allowing Zephyrian policymakers to gauge progress and identify areas needing improvement.

The Celebration of Diversity in Zephyria's LGBTQ Community

In Zephyria, the LGBTQ community embodies a vibrant celebration of diversity that is intricately woven into the fabric of its society. This celebration is not merely a passive acknowledgment of differences; it is an active, dynamic process that fosters inclusivity, acceptance, and a sense of belonging among its members. The celebration of diversity in Zephyria's LGBTQ community can be understood through several key theoretical frameworks, including intersectionality, social constructivism, and the concept of community resilience.

Theoretical Frameworks

Intersectionality serves as a foundational theory for understanding the complexities within the LGBTQ community in Zephyria. Coined by Kimberlé Crenshaw, intersectionality posits that individuals experience overlapping social identities, which can lead to unique modes of discrimination and privilege. In Zephyria, the LGBTQ community encompasses a multitude of identities, including race, ethnicity, gender, and socioeconomic status. This multiplicity is celebrated through various cultural events and initiatives that highlight the unique experiences of individuals at these intersections. For example, the annual Zephyrian Pride Festival showcases not only LGBTQ identities but also the diverse backgrounds of its participants, featuring performances, art, and discussions that reflect the community's rich tapestry.

Social constructivism further illuminates the ways in which identity and diversity are constructed and negotiated within Zephyria. This theory emphasizes that identities are not static but are shaped by social contexts and interactions. In

Zephyria, the LGBTQ community actively engages in dialogues that challenge normative definitions of identity. For instance, the Zephyrian LGBTQ Alliance hosts workshops that encourage participants to explore and express their identities in ways that transcend traditional binaries. This approach fosters a culture of acceptance and self-expression, enabling individuals to celebrate their uniqueness while finding solidarity with others.

Community resilience is another crucial lens through which to view the celebration of diversity in Zephyria. Resilience refers to the ability of a community to adapt and thrive in the face of challenges. The LGBTQ community in Zephyria has demonstrated remarkable resilience by creating safe spaces and support networks that empower individuals to embrace their identities. One notable example is the establishment of the Rainbow Resource Center, which provides resources, counseling, and social events for LGBTQ individuals and their allies. This center not only serves as a refuge but also as a hub for celebrating diversity through art exhibits, storytelling nights, and cultural exchanges.

Cultural Events and Initiatives

The celebration of diversity in Zephyria is epitomized by various cultural events and initiatives that promote LGBTQ visibility and acceptance. The **Zephyrian Pride Festival**, held annually, is a vibrant showcase of LGBTQ culture and identity. This festival features a parade that winds through the heart of the city, where participants don colorful attire, wave flags, and chant slogans advocating for equality and acceptance. The festival also includes workshops, panel discussions, and performances by LGBTQ artists, providing a platform for voices that are often marginalized.

In addition to Pride, the **Diversity Month** in Zephyria is a month-long celebration dedicated to honoring the various identities within the LGBTQ community. During this month, local businesses, schools, and organizations participate by hosting events that highlight different aspects of LGBTQ culture. For instance, art galleries feature exhibitions by LGBTQ artists, while schools implement educational programs that focus on LGBTQ history and issues. This initiative not only raises awareness but also fosters inter-community dialogue, allowing individuals from different backgrounds to learn from one another.

Challenges and Progress

Despite the progressive nature of Zephyria's LGBTQ community, challenges remain. Issues such as discrimination, stigma, and the need for intersectional representation continue to surface. For example, while the Pride Festival is a celebration of diversity, it has faced criticism for not adequately representing the voices of LGBTQ individuals of color. Activists within the community have worked tirelessly to address these concerns, advocating for more inclusive programming and representation in leadership roles within LGBTQ organizations.

Furthermore, the celebration of diversity in Zephyria is also reflected in its legislative efforts. The government has implemented policies aimed at protecting the rights of LGBTQ individuals, such as anti-discrimination laws and healthcare access initiatives. However, the effectiveness of these policies is often contingent upon community engagement and activism, highlighting the ongoing need for vigilance and advocacy.

Conclusion

In conclusion, the celebration of diversity in Zephyria's LGBTQ community is a multifaceted phenomenon that encompasses cultural events, theoretical frameworks, and ongoing challenges. Through intersectional approaches, social constructivist practices, and resilient community-building efforts, Zephyria stands as a model for how societies can embrace and celebrate the rich diversity within their LGBTQ populations. As the community continues to evolve, the commitment to inclusivity and acceptance remains a cornerstone of Zephyrian identity, fostering an environment where all individuals can thrive authentically.

The Impact of LGBTQ Movements on Zephyria's Society

The LGBTQ movements in Zephyria have profoundly shaped the social fabric and cultural landscape of the society. Rooted in the foundational principles of equality and social justice, these movements have not only advocated for the rights of LGBTQ individuals but have also influenced broader societal norms and values. This section will explore the multifaceted impact of LGBTQ activism on Zephyria, highlighting its contributions to social change, identity formation, and community resilience.

Social Change and Legal Reforms

One of the most significant impacts of the LGBTQ movements in Zephyria has been the advancement of legal reforms aimed at ensuring equal rights and protections for LGBTQ individuals. Activists have successfully lobbied for legislation that recognizes same-sex marriages, prohibits discrimination based on sexual orientation and gender identity, and provides comprehensive anti-bullying measures in educational institutions.

The legal framework established by these movements has been instrumental in fostering an environment of acceptance and inclusivity. For instance, the landmark case of *Zephyria v. The State* (Year) set a precedent by affirming the rights of same-sex couples to adopt children, a decision that not only benefited LGBTQ families but also challenged traditional notions of family structures in Zephyrian society.

Cultural Acceptance and Representation

Beyond legal reforms, LGBTQ movements in Zephyria have significantly contributed to cultural acceptance and representation. Through pride parades, art exhibitions, and media campaigns, LGBTQ activists have raised awareness about the diversity of sexual orientations and gender identities.

The annual Zephyria Pride Festival, for example, has become a vibrant celebration of LGBTQ culture, attracting participants from all walks of life. The festival serves as a platform for LGBTQ artists, performers, and speakers to share their stories and experiences, fostering a sense of community and belonging. Moreover, the visibility of LGBTQ individuals in mainstream media has challenged stereotypes and promoted positive representations, thereby normalizing diverse identities in the public consciousness.

Identity Formation and Intersectionality

The impact of LGBTQ movements on identity formation in Zephyria cannot be overstated. Activism has empowered individuals to embrace their sexual and gender identities openly, leading to a greater understanding of the complexities of identity.

The concept of intersectionality, as articulated by theorists such as Kimberlé Crenshaw, has been particularly influential in Zephyria. Activists have highlighted the interconnectedness of various identities, including race, class, and disability, within the LGBTQ community. This recognition has led to more inclusive activism that addresses the unique challenges faced by marginalized groups within the LGBTQ spectrum. For instance, the formation of the *Zephyria Coalition for Intersectional Justice* has brought together diverse voices to advocate for policies that address the specific needs of LGBTQ individuals of color and those with disabilities.

Community Resilience and Support Networks

The resilience of the LGBTQ community in Zephyria can be attributed to the support networks established through activism. Organizations such as *Zephyr LGBTQ Center* and *Pride Alliance* provide essential services, including mental health support, legal assistance, and safe spaces for LGBTQ individuals.

These networks have been crucial in fostering a sense of belonging and solidarity among community members, particularly during challenging times. For example, during the recent economic downturn, these organizations mobilized resources to provide financial assistance to LGBTQ individuals disproportionately affected by job losses. The collective action taken by these groups exemplifies the strength and unity of the LGBTQ community in Zephyria.

Challenges and Ongoing Struggles

Despite the progress achieved, the LGBTQ movements in Zephyria continue to face challenges. Issues such as transphobia, discrimination in healthcare, and violence against LGBTQ individuals remain prevalent. Activists are actively working to address these issues through awareness campaigns and advocacy for policy changes.

Moreover, the rise of conservative backlash against LGBTQ rights poses a significant threat to the advancements made. This resistance underscores the importance of ongoing activism and community engagement to safeguard the rights and dignity of LGBTQ individuals in Zephyria.

Conclusion

In conclusion, the LGBTQ movements in Zephyria have had a transformative impact on society, driving social change, fostering cultural acceptance, and promoting resilience within the community. The interplay of activism and identity has not only empowered LGBTQ individuals but has also enriched the broader societal landscape, making Zephyria a more inclusive and equitable society. As the movements continue to evolve, their influence will undoubtedly shape the future of Zephyria, paving the way for further advancements in human rights and social justice.

Lessons and Inspirations from Zephyria's LGBTQ Activism

The LGBTQ movements in Zephyria serve as a beacon of hope and a source of inspiration for activists and communities around the world. This section explores the key lessons learned from Zephyria's approach to LGBTQ activism and the broader implications for identity politics and social justice.

The Power of Inclusion

One of the most significant lessons from Zephyria is the power of inclusion in activism. The foundational principles of equality and social justice in Zephyria emphasize that true progress cannot be achieved without the active participation of all community members. This inclusivity fosters a sense of belonging and empowerment, allowing individuals from diverse backgrounds to contribute their unique perspectives and experiences.

$$\text{Inclusion} = \frac{\text{Diversity} + \text{Representation}}{\text{Barriers to Participation}} \tag{11}$$

In this equation, the numerator represents the necessity of diverse voices and representation within the LGBTQ community, while the denominator signifies the barriers that must be dismantled to facilitate participation. Zephyria's LGBTQ activism exemplifies how dismantling these barriers leads to a more robust and effective movement.

The Role of Education and Awareness

Zephyria's commitment to education as a tool for activism cannot be overstated. Through workshops, community events, and educational campaigns, activists in Zephyria have successfully raised awareness about LGBTQ issues, rights, and history. This emphasis on education has led to a more informed populace that is better equipped to challenge discrimination and advocate for equality.

$$\text{Awareness} = \text{Education} \times \text{Engagement} \tag{12}$$

In this context, awareness is a product of both education and community engagement. Zephyria's model illustrates that when individuals are educated about LGBTQ issues and actively engaged in discussions, they are more likely to become allies and advocates for change.

Intersectionality in Activism

Zephyria's LGBTQ movements have also highlighted the importance of intersectionality in activism. Recognizing that individuals possess multiple identities that intersect—such as race, gender, class, and sexuality—activists in

Zephyria strive to address the unique challenges faced by marginalized groups within the LGBTQ community. This intersectional approach ensures that activism is not one-dimensional and that the voices of the most vulnerable are amplified.

$$\text{Intersectionality} = \sum_{i=1}^{n} \text{Identity}_i \tag{13}$$

Here, intersectionality is represented as the sum of various identities, illustrating that each identity contributes to the overall experience of oppression or privilege. Zephyria's LGBTQ activism demonstrates that by recognizing and addressing these intersections, movements can become more effective and equitable.

Community Building and Solidarity

The resilience of the LGBTQ community in Zephyria is rooted in its emphasis on community building and solidarity. Activists have created networks of support that not only address immediate needs but also foster long-term relationships and collaborations. These networks serve as safe spaces for individuals to share their experiences, seek advice, and mobilize for collective action.

$$\text{Solidarity} = \text{Support} + \text{Collective Action} \tag{14}$$

This equation highlights that solidarity is achieved through both emotional support and coordinated efforts toward common goals. The strong sense of community in Zephyria has been pivotal in overcoming challenges and advancing LGBTQ rights.

Celebrating Diversity

Finally, Zephyria's LGBTQ movements underscore the importance of celebrating diversity. Events such as Pride parades and cultural festivals not only serve as platforms for advocacy but also celebrate the richness of LGBTQ identities. This celebration fosters pride and visibility, countering stigma and discrimination.

$$\text{Visibility} = \text{Celebration} \times \text{Representation} \tag{15}$$

In this equation, visibility is enhanced through the celebration of diverse identities and the representation of those identities in public spaces. Zephyria's commitment to celebrating diversity has proven to be a powerful tool for fostering acceptance and understanding.

Conclusion

The lessons and inspirations drawn from Zephyria's LGBTQ activism offer valuable insights for movements worldwide. By prioritizing inclusion, education, intersectionality, community building, and celebration, activists can create more effective and equitable movements. The experiences of Zephyria remind us that the fight for LGBTQ rights is not just about legal recognition but also about fostering a society where all individuals can thrive authentically and without fear.

Chapter Three: The Post-Apocalyptic Society of Apolonia

The Collapse of Apolonia's Civilization

Causes and Consequences of the Collapse

The collapse of Apolonia's civilization is a multifaceted event that can be attributed to a combination of environmental, social, and political factors. Understanding these causes not only sheds light on the specific events that led to the downfall of this society but also offers insights into the broader implications for identity and activism within post-apocalyptic contexts.

Environmental Factors

One of the primary causes of the collapse was the severe environmental degradation that Apolonia faced. Overexploitation of natural resources, such as deforestation and unsustainable agricultural practices, led to significant ecological imbalances. According to the *Environmental Degradation Theory*, societies that fail to manage their natural resources sustainably risk facing catastrophic consequences. In Apolonia, the depletion of arable land resulted in widespread famine, which created a desperate populace that struggled to survive.

The following equation illustrates the relationship between resource depletion and societal stability:

$$S = \frac{R}{D} \tag{16}$$

where S represents societal stability, R is the available resources, and D is the demand for those resources. As resources diminished, the stability of Apolonia's society decreased, leading to civil unrest and eventual collapse.

Social Fragmentation

In addition to environmental challenges, social fragmentation played a significant role in the collapse of Apolonia. The once-cohesive society became divided along class and identity lines, exacerbated by the scarcity of resources. The *Social Identity Theory* posits that individuals derive a sense of self from their group memberships, and in times of crisis, this can lead to heightened in-group versus out-group dynamics.

As resources became scarce, competition among various social groups intensified. Marginalized communities, including the LGBTQ population, faced increased discrimination and violence, which further fractured societal cohesion. The lack of solidarity among different identity groups weakened collective action, making it difficult to mount a unified response to the crisis.

Political Corruption and Mismanagement

Political corruption and mismanagement were also critical factors that contributed to the collapse. The leadership of Apolonia failed to address the growing disparities and environmental challenges, often prioritizing personal gain over the welfare of the populace. This aligns with the *Corruption and Governance Theory*, which suggests that corruption undermines public trust and leads to ineffective governance.

The government's inability to implement effective policies for resource management and social equity resulted in widespread disillusionment. Protests erupted, but rather than addressing the root causes of dissent, the ruling elite resorted to repression, further alienating the populace. The equation below illustrates the relationship between governance quality and social unrest:

$$U = \frac{G}{C} \qquad (17)$$

where U is the level of unrest, G represents governance quality, and C is the level of corruption. As governance quality declined due to corruption, unrest escalated, contributing to the eventual collapse of Apolonia.

Consequences of the Collapse

The consequences of the collapse were profound and far-reaching. The immediate aftermath saw a breakdown of social order, leading to chaos and violence. Survival became the primary concern, and individuals and groups resorted to various strategies to navigate the new reality.

For the LGBTQ community, the collapse meant a regression in rights and recognition. In the absence of a stable government, many LGBTQ individuals faced increased violence and discrimination, as societal norms shifted towards survival at any cost. The lack of legal protections led to the formation of underground networks, where individuals sought safety and community outside of the traditional societal structures.

The collapse also had long-term implications for identity formation in Apolonia. As people struggled to survive, they began to redefine their identities in relation to the new social dynamics. The concept of identity became fluid, influenced by the necessity of adaptability in a harsh environment.

Conclusion

In summary, the collapse of Apolonia was the result of a complex interplay of environmental degradation, social fragmentation, and political corruption. The consequences of this collapse not only transformed the landscape of Apolonia but also reshaped the identities of its inhabitants, particularly marginalized groups like the LGBTQ community. Understanding these dynamics is crucial for analyzing the role of activism in the rebuilding efforts that followed the collapse, as individuals sought to reclaim their identities and rights in a radically changed society.

Survival and Recovery Efforts in Apolonia

The collapse of Apolonia's civilization was not merely a catastrophic event but a profound rupture that reshaped the very fabric of its society. In the aftermath, survival and recovery became paramount for the remnants of its population. This section explores the multifaceted efforts undertaken by the inhabitants of Apolonia to navigate the challenges of their new reality, focusing on community resilience, resource management, and the role of identity in the recovery process.

Community Resilience and Social Structures

The initial phase of survival in Apolonia was characterized by a return to basic communal living. With the collapse of centralized governance, local communities emerged as the primary units of organization. These communities were often formed around shared identities, whether based on geography, ethnicity, or gender. The theory of *social capital*, as posited by Bourdieu (1986), became crucial in understanding how relationships and networks facilitated cooperation and resource sharing.

$$C = \sum_{i=1}^{n} \frac{1}{d_i} \tag{18}$$

Where C represents the community's social capital, n is the number of individuals, and d_i is the degree of connection each individual has within the community. Higher social capital allowed for more effective collaboration, which was essential in the face of scarcity.

Resource Management and Sustainability

In the wake of the collapse, resource scarcity became a pressing issue. The inhabitants of Apolonia had to innovate in their approaches to resource management. Traditional agricultural practices were often abandoned in favor of permaculture and community gardens, which promoted sustainability and resilience. The concept of *ecological resilience*, described by Holling (1973), played a significant role in these efforts.

$$R = \frac{S}{D} \tag{19}$$

Where R is resilience, S is the system's stability, and D is the degree of disturbance. Communities that adapted their practices to the new ecological realities were able to maintain a semblance of stability, allowing for the gradual rebuilding of their society.

Identity and Collective Memory

The recovery efforts in Apolonia were also deeply intertwined with issues of identity and collective memory. As communities struggled to redefine themselves in the aftermath of collapse, they often turned to narratives of their past to foster a sense of belonging and purpose. The theory of *collective memory*, as articulated by

Halbwachs (1992), emphasizes how groups remember their pasts in ways that shape their identities and social cohesion.

In Apolonia, storytelling became a vital tool for healing. Elders shared tales of resilience and survival, which not only preserved cultural heritage but also inspired hope among the younger generations. This process of remembering was not without challenges, as differing narratives often led to tensions within and between communities. However, the act of remembering served as a unifying force, allowing individuals to connect with a shared history.

Challenges to Recovery

Despite these efforts, the path to recovery was fraught with challenges. The ongoing threat of violence, resource depletion, and the psychological toll of the collapse created an atmosphere of uncertainty. Many communities faced internal conflicts, often exacerbated by differing priorities and ideologies regarding recovery strategies. The theory of *adaptive capacity*, as defined by Folke et al. (2002), became relevant here, as it highlights the ability of communities to adjust to changing circumstances.

$$A = \frac{R}{C} \qquad (20)$$

Where A is adaptive capacity, R is resilience, and C is the complexity of the social system. Communities that could navigate these complexities while maintaining resilience were more likely to succeed in their recovery efforts.

Conclusion

In conclusion, the survival and recovery efforts in Apolonia represent a complex interplay of community resilience, resource management, and identity formation. While the challenges were significant, the inhabitants' ability to adapt and innovate was a testament to their resilience. The lessons learned from Apolonia's recovery efforts provide valuable insights into the broader themes of activism and identity within the context of post-apocalyptic societies. As the communities of Apolonia continue to rebuild, their stories of survival and solidarity serve as a reminder of the enduring power of human connection in the face of adversity.

Identity Formation in the Post-Apocalyptic Society

In the aftermath of the collapse of Apolonia's civilization, identity formation becomes a multifaceted process shaped by the remnants of pre-apocalyptic norms and the exigencies of survival in a radically altered social landscape. This section explores the dynamics of identity formation in Apolonia, drawing on relevant theories and examples to illustrate the complexities faced by individuals and communities as they navigate their new realities.

Theoretical Frameworks

Identity formation is often understood through various theoretical lenses, including social constructivism, intersectionality, and post-structuralism. Social constructivism posits that identities are not inherent or fixed but are constructed through social interactions and cultural contexts. This perspective is particularly relevant in a post-apocalyptic society, where traditional social structures have been dismantled, and individuals must renegotiate their identities in response to new social realities.

Intersectionality, a concept coined by Kimberlé Crenshaw, emphasizes that identities are not singular but are instead shaped by overlapping social categories such as race, gender, sexuality, and class. In Apolonia, where survival often hinges on collaboration and mutual support, individuals may find their identities redefined by their roles within new social networks that prioritize these intersecting identities.

Post-structuralism further complicates the understanding of identity by suggesting that identities are fluid and contingent, constantly in flux as individuals navigate various social contexts. This fluidity is particularly pronounced in a post-apocalyptic setting, where individuals may adopt multiple identities based on their immediate needs and the evolving social landscape.

Challenges to Identity Formation

In the chaotic environment of Apolonia, identity formation faces several challenges. The collapse of societal norms leads to a crisis of identity for many individuals. Without the guiding frameworks of pre-apocalyptic society, individuals must grapple with questions of self-worth, belonging, and purpose. The absence of established roles can result in identity fragmentation, where individuals struggle to reconcile their past identities with their current realities.

Moreover, the trauma associated with the collapse can significantly impact identity formation. Survivors may experience a profound sense of loss, not only of loved ones but also of the social structures that once provided stability. This trauma can manifest in various ways, including anxiety, depression, and a pervasive sense of disconnection from one's previous identity. The psychological theories of identity, such as Erik Erikson's stages of psychosocial development, suggest that identity formation is deeply influenced by social relationships and the ability to navigate crises. In Apolonia, the lack of stable relationships further complicates this process.

Examples of Identity Formation in Apolonia

Despite these challenges, individuals and communities in Apolonia demonstrate remarkable resilience in their identity formation processes. For example, the emergence of support networks among LGBTQ individuals illustrates how shared experiences of marginalization can foster a sense of belonging and collective identity. These networks often prioritize inclusivity and mutual aid, allowing individuals to redefine their identities in ways that affirm their experiences and values.

Consider the case of the "Rainbow Coalition," a grassroots organization formed in the aftermath of the collapse. This coalition brings together LGBTQ individuals and allies to advocate for rights, provide emotional support, and facilitate resource sharing. Members of the coalition report that their involvement has helped them reclaim their identities, transforming feelings of isolation into a sense of community and purpose. This collective identity is rooted in shared struggles and aspirations, illustrating how identity can be reconstructed in the face of adversity.

Additionally, the concept of "survivor identity" emerges as a significant theme in Apolonia. Many individuals adopt this identity as a means of coping with their experiences and asserting their agency in a world that often feels chaotic and unpredictable. The narrative of survival becomes a powerful tool for identity formation, allowing individuals to find meaning in their experiences and connect with others who share similar struggles.

Conclusion

In conclusion, identity formation in the post-apocalyptic society of Apolonia is a complex and dynamic process influenced by theoretical frameworks, challenges, and examples of resilience. As individuals navigate the remnants of their former identities and confront the realities of their new existence, they engage in a continual process of negotiation and redefinition. The interplay of social constructs, trauma, and community support shapes the identities of individuals in Apolonia, highlighting the importance of activism and solidarity in the face of adversity. The journey of identity formation in Apolonia serves as a testament to the human capacity for resilience and adaptation, even in the most challenging of circumstances.

The Role of Activism in Rebuilding Apolonia

In the aftermath of the collapse of Apolonia, the significance of activism emerged as a critical force in the reconstruction of societal norms, values, and infrastructures. Activism in this post-apocalyptic context can be understood through the lens of several theoretical frameworks, including social constructivism, resilience theory, and intersectionality. Each of these frameworks provides a unique perspective on how communities mobilize to address the challenges posed by the collapse and how they redefine identity and social structures in the process.

Theoretical Frameworks

Social Constructivism posits that our understanding of reality is shaped through social interactions and shared experiences. In Apolonia, the collective trauma from the collapse led to a re-evaluation of identities. Activists began to engage in dialogue that allowed for the reconstruction of social narratives, emphasizing the importance of shared experiences in fostering a sense of community. This is exemplified by the formation of grassroots organizations that sought to document the stories of marginalized groups, including LGBTQ individuals, thereby validating their experiences and identities within the new societal framework.

Resilience Theory highlights the ability of communities to adapt and recover from adversity. In the context of Apolonia, activism became a tool for resilience. Activists organized mutual aid networks that provided essential resources, such as food, shelter, and medical care. For instance, the "Apolonian Collective" emerged as a prominent organization that not only addressed immediate survival needs but also facilitated discussions around long-term recovery strategies. Their work illustrated how activism could foster resilience by empowering individuals to take agency over their circumstances.

Intersectionality plays a crucial role in understanding the diverse experiences within the LGBTQ community in Apolonia. Activists recognized that the collapse did not affect all individuals equally; factors such as race, gender, and socioeconomic status compounded the challenges faced by many. By adopting an intersectional approach, activists worked to ensure that the voices of the most marginalized were included in the rebuilding process. This led to the establishment of inclusive forums where individuals could share their unique experiences and advocate for policies that addressed their specific needs.

Challenges Faced by Activists

Despite the pivotal role of activism in rebuilding Apolonia, activists encountered numerous challenges. The initial chaos following the collapse created an environment of distrust and fragmentation. Many individuals were hesitant to engage with activist groups due to past experiences of oppression or fear of retribution. Furthermore, the scarcity of resources often led to competition among groups, undermining the potential for collaboration.

A notable example of these challenges can be seen in the struggle for recognition of LGBTQ rights. Activists faced resistance from factions that sought to impose traditional values, viewing LGBTQ identities as a threat to the newly forming societal norms. This tension highlighted the need for activists to navigate complex social dynamics while advocating for inclusivity.

Examples of Activism in Action

One prominent example of activism in post-apocalyptic Apolonia is the "Rainbow Rebuild" initiative, which aimed to create safe spaces for LGBTQ individuals. This initiative emerged in response to the increased vulnerability of LGBTQ individuals in the aftermath of the collapse. Activists organized workshops that provided both practical skills for survival and discussions on identity and community building. These workshops not only empowered participants but also fostered a sense of belonging and solidarity among diverse groups.

Additionally, the "Voices of Apolonia" campaign utilized storytelling as a form of activism. By collecting and sharing narratives from LGBTQ individuals, the campaign sought to humanize the struggles faced by this community and challenge prevailing stereotypes. This initiative not only raised awareness but also built empathy among the broader population, promoting a more inclusive perspective in the rebuilding process.

The Impact of Activism on Society

The impact of activism in Apolonia's rebuilding efforts cannot be overstated. Through their efforts, activists catalyzed significant changes in societal attitudes towards LGBTQ individuals. The establishment of community centers that provided resources and support for LGBTQ individuals served as a testament to the power of activism in fostering acceptance and understanding.

Furthermore, the collaboration between different activist groups led to the creation of a more cohesive society. By emphasizing intersectionality and inclusivity, activists were able to bridge divides and unite various factions within Apolonia. This collective effort not only facilitated the rebuilding of physical structures but also laid the groundwork for a more equitable and just society.

Conclusion

In conclusion, the role of activism in rebuilding Apolonia was multifaceted and transformative. Through the application of social constructivism, resilience theory, and intersectionality, activists were able to navigate the complexities of a post-apocalyptic society. Despite facing significant challenges, their efforts led to the establishment of inclusive spaces and the promotion of diverse identities. The examples of the "Rainbow Rebuild" initiative and the "Voices of Apolonia" campaign illustrate the profound impact of activism on both individual lives and societal structures. As Apolonia continues to evolve, the legacy of activism will remain a cornerstone of its journey towards recovery and renewal.

The LGBTQ Movements in Apolonia

LGBTQ Challenges and Discrimination After the Collapse

In the aftermath of the catastrophic collapse of Apolonia, the LGBTQ community faced unprecedented challenges and discrimination that were exacerbated by the chaotic socio-political landscape. The collapse not only dismantled the existing societal structures but also stripped away the hard-won rights and protections that LGBTQ individuals had fought for prior to the apocalypse. This section explores the multifaceted challenges faced by LGBTQ individuals in Apolonia, drawing on relevant theories of identity, oppression, and resilience.

Theoretical Framework

To understand the challenges faced by LGBTQ individuals in a post-apocalyptic society, we can employ intersectionality theory, which posits that individuals experience oppression in overlapping and interdependent ways based on their identities (Crenshaw, 1989). In Apolonia, the collapse created a new hierarchy of survival, where identities that were once celebrated became sources of vulnerability. The intersection of sexual orientation, gender identity, and socio-economic status shaped the experiences of LGBTQ individuals, leading to unique challenges that were often overlooked by mainstream survival narratives.

Discrimination in Resource Allocation

One of the primary challenges faced by LGBTQ individuals in Apolonia was discrimination in access to essential resources. In the wake of the collapse, resources became scarce, and survival often hinged on forming alliances and networks. However, LGBTQ individuals frequently found themselves marginalized within these networks. For instance, a study conducted by the Apolonian Institute of Social Research (AISR) in 2045 revealed that LGBTQ individuals were 40% less likely to receive food and shelter assistance compared to their heterosexual counterparts. This disparity was rooted in deep-seated prejudices that resurfaced in times of crisis, as survival instincts often led to the prioritization of perceived "traditional" family units over LGBTQ individuals.

Violence and Intimidation

The collapse of social order also resulted in a surge of violence and intimidation directed toward LGBTQ individuals. According to a report by the Coalition for LGBTQ Rights in Apolonia (CLRAP), incidents of hate crimes increased by 150% in the first year following the collapse. The breakdown of law enforcement and community safety structures created an environment where LGBTQ individuals were particularly vulnerable to violence. Many were forced to conceal their identities to avoid targeted attacks, leading to a pervasive culture of fear.

Mental Health Crisis

The psychological toll of living in a hostile environment cannot be overstated. The collapse brought about not only physical survival challenges but also a mental health crisis among LGBTQ individuals. The loss of community support systems, coupled with the stress of discrimination and violence, led to increased rates of anxiety, depression, and PTSD. A study published in the Journal of Post-Apocalyptic Psychology (JPAP) indicated that LGBTQ individuals reported mental health issues at rates 60% higher than their non-LGBTQ peers. This mental health crisis was compounded by the lack of accessible mental health resources in the post-collapse landscape.

Resilience and Resistance

Despite these challenges, the LGBTQ community in Apolonia exhibited remarkable resilience and resistance. Grassroots organizations began to emerge, focusing on mutual aid and support networks. For example, the group "Rainbow Resilience" formed in 2046, providing safe spaces for LGBTQ individuals to share resources, skills, and emotional support. This initiative not only addressed immediate survival needs but also fostered a sense of community and belonging.

Moreover, the LGBTQ community became increasingly involved in advocacy efforts to challenge discrimination and violence. Activists organized protests and awareness campaigns, emphasizing the need for inclusive policies in the rebuilding of Apolonia. These efforts were grounded in the recognition that the fight for LGBTQ rights is integral to the broader struggle for justice and equality in society.

Conclusion

The challenges and discrimination faced by LGBTQ individuals in post-apocalyptic Apolonia illustrate the complexities of identity and oppression in times of crisis. Through the lens of intersectionality, we can see how the collapse of societal structures amplified existing prejudices and created new barriers to survival. However, the resilience and resistance of the LGBTQ community also highlight the potential for solidarity and activism in the face of adversity. As Apolonia begins to rebuild, it is crucial to ensure that the voices and experiences of LGBTQ individuals are included in the discourse on recovery and social justice.

Bibliography

[1] Crenshaw, K. (1989). *Demarginalizing the Intersection of Race and Sex: A Black Feminist Critique of Antidiscrimination Doctrine, Feminist Theory and Antiracist Politics.* University of Chicago Legal Forum.

[2] Apolonian Institute of Social Research. (2045). *Resource Allocation and Inequality in Post-Collapse Apolonia.*

[3] Coalition for LGBTQ Rights in Apolonia. (2046). *Annual Report on Hate Crimes and Discrimination Against LGBTQ Individuals.*

[4] Journal of Post-Apocalyptic Psychology. (2047). *Mental Health in the Wake of Societal Collapse: A Study of LGBTQ Individuals.*

LGBTQ Survival Strategies and Support Networks

In the post-apocalyptic society of Apolonia, LGBTQ individuals faced unprecedented challenges, including rampant discrimination, violence, and the struggle for basic human rights. The collapse of traditional social structures necessitated the emergence of innovative survival strategies and robust support networks to ensure the safety and well-being of LGBTQ individuals. These strategies can be categorized into three primary areas: community building, resource sharing, and advocacy.

Community Building

The formation of safe spaces became a critical survival strategy for LGBTQ individuals in Apolonia. As conventional societal norms disintegrated, marginalized groups sought refuge in informal communities where they could express their identities freely. These safe spaces often took the form of underground gatherings, secret meeting places, and virtual networks that provided emotional support and camaraderie.

Example: The Rainbow Haven was established as a clandestine refuge where LGBTQ individuals could gather without fear of persecution. The Haven provided not only a physical space but also a sense of belonging and solidarity. Regular meetings fostered a strong community identity, allowing members to share experiences, strategies, and resources.

Resource Sharing

In a society struggling with scarcity, resource sharing became vital for survival. LGBTQ individuals and allies created networks to exchange essential supplies, from food and clothing to medical care and emotional support. These networks often operated on the principles of mutual aid, emphasizing collective responsibility and solidarity.

Theory: Mutual Aid Theory posits that communities can thrive through cooperative efforts, particularly in times of crisis. This theory underpinned many of the resource-sharing initiatives in Apolonia, as LGBTQ individuals banded together to ensure that no one was left behind.

Example: The Supply Chain Initiative was a grassroots movement that connected LGBTQ individuals with surplus resources from sympathetic allies. By establishing a barter system, members could trade goods and services, thereby alleviating some of the burdens imposed by the post-apocalyptic conditions.

Advocacy

Advocacy played a crucial role in the survival of LGBTQ individuals in Apolonia. Activists worked tirelessly to raise awareness about the unique challenges faced by the community and to push for recognition and rights in the new societal order.

Challenges: The primary obstacle to advocacy in Apolonia was the pervasive stigma surrounding LGBTQ identities. Many individuals feared retaliation or ostracization, which stifled open discussions about rights and recognition. Additionally, the lack of a formal political structure made it difficult to enact change through traditional channels.

Example: The Coalition for LGBTQ Rights emerged as a vocal advocate for the community, organizing protests and awareness campaigns. Their slogan, *"Visibility is Survival,"* encapsulated their mission to ensure that LGBTQ individuals were seen and heard in a society that often rendered them invisible.

The Impact of Support Networks

The survival strategies employed by LGBTQ individuals in Apolonia not only provided immediate relief but also laid the groundwork for a more inclusive society. The solidarity forged within these support networks contributed to a sense of resilience and empowerment, allowing LGBTQ individuals to navigate the challenges of their environment with greater confidence.

Conclusion: The survival strategies and support networks developed by the LGBTQ community in Apolonia exemplify the strength of human connection in the face of adversity. By fostering community, sharing resources, and advocating for rights, LGBTQ individuals not only survived but also began to thrive in a world that sought to marginalize them. These efforts serve as a testament to the enduring power of identity and activism in shaping a more equitable future.

$$\text{Survival Success} = f(\text{Community Building, Resource Sharing, Advocacy}) \quad (21)$$

The Fight for LGBTQ Rights and Recognition

In the post-apocalyptic society of Apolonia, the struggle for LGBTQ rights and recognition has emerged as a critical focal point in the broader narrative of survival and recovery. The collapse of civilization brought about not only physical devastation but also a regression in social norms and rights, making the fight for LGBTQ recognition a matter of both identity and existence. This section explores the theoretical frameworks underpinning this struggle, the unique challenges faced by the LGBTQ community in Apolonia, and the various strategies employed to combat discrimination and advocate for rights.

Theoretical Frameworks

The fight for LGBTQ rights in Apolonia can be analyzed through several theoretical lenses, including intersectionality, social justice theory, and post-colonial theory.

Intersectionality posits that individuals experience multiple, overlapping identities that can lead to unique forms of discrimination and privilege. In Apolonia, the LGBTQ community is not a monolith; various identities intersect—such as race, class, and gender—compounding the challenges they face. For example, a queer person of color may experience discrimination not only based on their sexual orientation but also due to their racial identity, leading to a more complex struggle for recognition and rights.

Social justice theory emphasizes the need for equitable treatment and the dismantling of oppressive structures. In the context of Apolonia, where societal norms have been upended, the LGBTQ community must navigate a landscape where traditional power dynamics have been disrupted but not eliminated. Activists draw upon social justice principles to advocate for policies that protect LGBTQ individuals from violence and discrimination.

Post-colonial theory provides insight into how historical narratives shape current identities and struggles. The remnants of pre-collapse societal norms often reflect colonial attitudes towards sexuality and gender. Activists in Apolonia must confront these legacies while forging new identities and rights frameworks that reflect their lived experiences.

Challenges Faced by the LGBTQ Community

The collapse of Apolonia's civilization resulted in a significant breakdown of social order, leading to an increase in violence and discrimination against marginalized groups. LGBTQ individuals face specific challenges, including:

- **Violence and Intimidation:** In a society struggling for survival, LGBTQ individuals often become targets of violence, as traditional gender roles are reasserted in an attempt to restore order. Reports of hate crimes against LGBTQ individuals have surged, with many fearing for their safety in public and private spaces.

- **Lack of Legal Protections:** The collapse of governmental structures has resulted in a vacuum of legal protections. LGBTQ individuals find themselves without recourse against discrimination, harassment, or violence. The absence of laws protecting their rights exacerbates their vulnerability and marginalization.

- **Social Stigma:** Cultural attitudes towards LGBTQ individuals have regressed in the aftermath of the collapse. Many communities view non-heteronormative identities as threats to societal stability, leading to widespread stigma and ostracism.

- **Resource Scarcity:** The dire economic conditions post-collapse have resulted in scarce resources for all, but LGBTQ individuals often find themselves at the bottom of the priority list for aid and support. This scarcity further complicates their ability to organize and advocate for their rights.

BIBLIOGRAPHY 69

Strategies for Advocacy and Recognition

Despite these challenges, the LGBTQ community in Apolonia has mobilized to fight for their rights and recognition through various strategies:

Community Building plays a crucial role in fostering resilience among LGBTQ individuals. By creating safe spaces for dialogue and support, community members can share their experiences and strategize collectively. Grassroots organizations have emerged, focusing on mutual aid, mental health support, and advocacy.

Coalition Building with other marginalized groups has proven effective in amplifying the voices of LGBTQ individuals. By aligning with feminist, anti-racist, and disability rights movements, LGBTQ activists can present a united front against oppression. This intersectional approach not only broadens the base of support but also highlights the interconnectedness of various struggles.

Public Awareness Campaigns are essential in challenging societal stigma and fostering acceptance. Activists have utilized storytelling, art, and public demonstrations to raise awareness about the issues faced by the LGBTQ community. These campaigns aim to educate the broader population and shift public perceptions.

Advocacy for Legal Protections is a critical component of the fight for rights. Activists are working to establish a framework for legal recognition of LGBTQ identities and protections against discrimination. This involves lobbying for the establishment of new governance structures that prioritize human rights and inclusivity.

Examples of Activism in Apolonia

Several notable initiatives exemplify the fight for LGBTQ rights in Apolonia:

- **The Rainbow Coalition:** A grassroots organization formed in the wake of the collapse, the Rainbow Coalition focuses on providing resources and support to LGBTQ individuals. They have organized community meetings, workshops, and outreach programs to raise awareness and foster solidarity.

- **The Pride March for Survival:** In a bold statement against oppression, LGBTQ activists organized a Pride march that emphasized survival and resilience. This event drew attention to the violence faced by the community and served as a platform for demands for recognition and rights.

- **The Safe Haven Initiative:** This initiative aims to create safe spaces for LGBTQ individuals fleeing violence or discrimination. By providing shelter and support, the Safe Haven Initiative has become a lifeline for many in the community.

In conclusion, the fight for LGBTQ rights and recognition in post-apocalyptic Apolonia is marked by resilience and determination. Despite facing significant challenges, the community continues to advocate for their rights, drawing upon various theoretical frameworks and strategies to navigate their unique struggles. The ongoing activism in Apolonia serves as a testament to the power of community and the enduring quest for dignity and recognition in the face of adversity.

The Role of LGBTQ Activism in Rebuilding Apolonia

The post-apocalyptic society of Apolonia presents a unique landscape for LGBTQ activism, characterized by both the remnants of a once-thriving civilization and the urgent need for social reconstruction. In this context, LGBTQ activism emerges not only as a means of advocating for rights and recognition but also as a crucial component in the broader efforts to rebuild social cohesion and community resilience.

Theoretical Framework

To understand the role of LGBTQ activism in this rebuilding process, we can draw upon the theories of social capital and collective identity. Pierre Bourdieu's concept of social capital emphasizes the importance of networks, relationships, and shared values in facilitating collective action (Bourdieu, 1986). In the fragmented society of Apolonia, LGBTQ activists leverage social capital to forge alliances with other marginalized groups, thereby enhancing their collective voice and influence.

Furthermore, Judith Butler's theory of performativity provides insight into how identity is constructed and expressed within the LGBTQ community. Butler posits that gender and sexual identities are not inherent but are performed through repeated actions and societal interactions (Butler, 1990). In the wake of societal collapse, the performance of LGBTQ identities becomes a powerful tool for resistance and reclamation, allowing individuals to assert their existence and rights in a world that seeks to erase them.

Challenges Faced by LGBTQ Activists

Despite the critical role of LGBTQ activism in rebuilding Apolonia, activists face significant challenges. The collapse of social structures has led to increased discrimination and violence against LGBTQ individuals, as traditional norms and protections have crumbled. Many activists report a resurgence of homophobic and transphobic sentiments, often exacerbated by the scarcity of resources and the struggle for survival.

Moreover, the fragmentation of communities poses a challenge to solidarity. As individuals prioritize survival, the focus on collective identity can wane, leading to a disconnection among LGBTQ individuals. This fragmentation complicates efforts to mobilize for rights and recognition, as activists must navigate a landscape where mutual support is often overshadowed by individual survival instincts.

Examples of Activism in Action

In response to these challenges, LGBTQ activists in Apolonia have developed innovative strategies to foster resilience and community support. One notable example is the establishment of "Safe Zones," which serve as both physical spaces and community networks where LGBTQ individuals can find refuge, support, and resources. These Safe Zones are often run by grassroots organizations that prioritize inclusivity and mutual aid, creating an environment where individuals can express their identities without fear of persecution.

Additionally, LGBTQ activists have engaged in public awareness campaigns to educate the broader community about the importance of diversity and inclusion. These campaigns often utilize storytelling as a tool for connection, allowing individuals to share their experiences and challenge prevailing stereotypes. By humanizing LGBTQ identities, activists aim to foster empathy and understanding, which are crucial for rebuilding social bonds.

The Impact of LGBTQ Activism on Rebuilding Efforts

The impact of LGBTQ activism extends beyond the immediate community; it plays a vital role in shaping the new societal values of Apolonia. As activists advocate for rights and recognition, they contribute to the establishment of a more inclusive and equitable society. This activism not only benefits LGBTQ individuals but also sets a precedent for the treatment of all marginalized groups within the rebuilding process.

Furthermore, the resilience demonstrated by LGBTQ activists serves as an inspiration for other communities facing similar struggles. By showcasing the power of collective action and solidarity, LGBTQ activism in Apolonia encourages a broader movement towards social justice and equality. This interconnectedness highlights the importance of intersectionality, as the fight for LGBTQ rights becomes intertwined with the struggles of other marginalized populations.

Conclusion

In conclusion, LGBTQ activism plays a pivotal role in the rebuilding of Apolonia, serving as both a means of advocacy and a catalyst for social cohesion. Despite facing numerous challenges, activists harness the power of social capital and collective identity to foster resilience and community support. Through innovative strategies and public awareness campaigns, LGBTQ activists not only assert their rights but also contribute to the development of a more inclusive society. The lessons learned from Apolonia's LGBTQ movements can serve as a blueprint for other communities navigating the complexities of post-apocalyptic recovery, emphasizing the need for solidarity, empathy, and intersectional advocacy in the pursuit of social justice.

Index

ability, 57, 59
absence, 55, 58
acceptance, 2, 4, 10, 11, 19, 26, 42–44, 46–48, 61
access, 17, 39, 46
achievement, 19
acknowledgment, 37, 38, 44
act, 57
action, 7, 10, 24, 30, 31, 48, 50, 54, 71
activism, 1–3, 5–12, 14–17, 19, 21, 22, 24, 26, 28, 29, 35, 44, 46, 48, 49, 53, 55, 57, 59–62, 64, 70, 71
activist, 61, 62
adaptability, 37, 55
adaptation, 41, 60
addition, 23
advancement, 46
adversity, 1, 4, 11, 21, 23, 24, 26, 31, 57, 59, 64, 70
advice, 50
advocacy, 8, 10, 12, 21, 23, 43, 44, 46, 48, 64, 65
advocate, 17, 24, 30, 59, 67, 70, 71
aftermath, 14, 19, 55, 57, 59–62
agency, 59
aid, 59, 66

anxiety, 58
apocalypse, 62
Apolonia, 1–4, 10–12, 53, 55, 57–62, 64–71
application, 62
approach, 8, 10, 37
array, 22
art, 21, 47
assistance, 48
attention, 18
authority, 16
awareness, 47, 48, 61, 64, 66, 71

backlash, 21, 23, 27, 35, 41, 48
balance, 39
beacon, 21, 26, 44
bedrock, 33
behavior, 36, 40
being, 65
belief, 14, 40, 42
belonging, 4, 11, 14, 38, 44, 47–49, 58, 59, 61
benefit, 33
bias, 34, 43
binary, 4, 38
blueprint, 35
book, 1, 5, 10
breakdown, 55, 68

73

bridge, 62
building, 11, 46, 50, 61, 65
burden, 10

camaraderie, 66
campaign, 61, 62
capacity, 60
care, 66
case, 3, 5, 10–12, 17, 20, 59
caste, 1
cataclysm, 13
catalyst, 2
catastrophe, 15
celebration, 10, 33, 37, 44, 46, 47
challenge, 12, 24, 36, 37, 61, 64, 71
change, 3, 5, 7, 10, 16, 17, 22, 24, 26, 29, 34, 39, 46, 48
chaos, 55, 61
civilization, 13, 53, 55, 57, 67, 68, 70
class, 10, 20, 24, 58
clothing, 66
coalition, 59
cohesion, 54, 70
collaboration, 58, 61, 62
collapse, 4, 11, 53, 55, 57–62, 64, 65, 67, 68, 71
collectivism, 36
color, 27, 38, 43, 46
combination, 35, 44, 53
commitment, 33, 35, 37, 43, 46
committee, 27
community, 1, 2, 4, 10, 11, 14–31, 35–38, 40–50, 55, 57, 59, 61, 62, 64–67, 69–71
competition, 54, 61
complacency, 36
complexity, 3, 8
component, 70

concept, 3, 8, 10, 15, 37, 38, 40, 44, 55, 58, 59
concern, 55
conclusion, 12, 15, 17, 28, 39, 41, 43, 46, 48, 57, 59, 62, 70
confidence, 67
conflict, 4, 15
confrontation, 18
connection, 57, 71
consciousness, 35, 47
construct, 3, 38
construction, 20
constructivism, 20, 37, 39, 40, 44, 58, 60, 62
context, 1, 2, 4, 11, 15, 39, 57, 60, 70
contingent, 46, 58
control, 17
cooperation, 35
cornerstone, 46, 62
corruption, 55
cost, 55
council, 14
counter, 21
crackdown, 18
creation, 11, 15, 62
creativity, 7
crisis, 54, 58, 64
criticism, 2, 46
critique, 41
culture, 11, 13, 15, 21, 47

day, 43
declaration, 19
defiance, 21
degradation, 55
demand, 21
depletion, 53
depression, 58
destination, 37

Index

determination, 19, 24, 26, 70
devastation, 67
development, 59
dialogue, 28, 37, 41
dichotomy, 20
dignity, 26, 48, 70
disarray, 17
disconnection, 58, 71
discourse, 21, 38, 64
discrimination, 10, 11, 15, 17, 20, 21, 25, 34, 38, 43, 45, 46, 48, 54, 55, 62, 64, 65, 67, 68, 71
disillusionment, 40, 41
dissemination, 11, 17
dissent, 16, 17, 21
distrust, 61
diversity, 4, 10, 33, 38, 39, 44, 46, 47, 71
document, 19
downfall, 53
downturn, 48
dynamic, 17, 37, 38, 41, 44, 59

education, 37, 38, 43
effectiveness, 10, 46
effort, 62
emergence, 1, 59, 65
empathy, 61, 71
emphasis, 37, 39, 50
employment, 17
empowerment, 11, 49, 67
enforcement, 34
engagement, 14, 35, 36, 46, 48
environment, 21, 35, 44, 46, 55, 58, 61, 67
equality, 7, 12, 15, 22, 24, 26, 33–35, 37, 39, 41–43, 46, 49, 64, 72

equation, 8, 14, 38, 39, 44, 50, 53
equity, 33
Erik Erikson's, 59
escapism, 41
essence, 26
establishment, 4, 10, 11, 17, 31, 36, 61, 62, 71
ethos, 3
event, 13, 18, 27, 53, 55
evolution, 15, 17, 41, 42
examination, 11
example, 2, 4, 11, 20, 21, 27, 35, 38, 46–48, 59, 61
exchange, 66
execution, 27
existence, 13, 41, 59, 67
expense, 39
experience, 8, 20, 26, 38, 43, 58
exploration, 3, 21, 27
expression, 4, 39

fabric, 4, 13, 37, 38, 43, 44, 46, 55
face, 2–5, 7, 10, 11, 19–21, 23, 24, 26, 29, 31, 43, 48, 57, 59, 64, 68, 70, 71
fairness, 33
fear, 21, 61
female, 20
festival, 27, 47
fight, 2, 10, 12, 22, 24, 26, 64, 67, 69, 70, 72
fluidity, 58
flux, 58
focus, 71
food, 36, 66
force, 22, 26, 57, 60
forefront, 35
form, 13, 41, 61, 65

formation, 4, 13–15, 19, 46, 47, 55, 57–59, 65
foster, 3, 10, 11, 28, 31, 37, 38, 50, 59, 71
fragmentation, 13, 55, 58, 61, 71
framework, 9, 19–21, 37–42
Fredric Jameson, 40
function, 38
future, 12, 19, 26, 35, 48

gain, 3, 12, 26
gender, 4, 10, 20, 24, 33, 42, 47, 58
generation, 37
governance, 1, 14–16, 36
government, 17–20, 41, 43, 46, 55
Gramsci, 15
groundwork, 62, 67
group, 21, 38

hand, 28
harassment, 11
harmony, 35, 37
healing, 57
health, 43
healthcare, 17, 43, 46, 48
hegemony, 15
Herbert Marcuse, 41
heritage, 57
history, 17–19, 57
homophobia, 8
hope, 21, 26, 31, 44, 57

idea, 38, 41
ideal, 14, 37, 39–41
idealism, 36, 40, 41
identity, 1, 3–5, 7, 9–15, 17, 19–21, 24, 26, 27, 30, 35, 37–39, 42, 44, 46–48, 53–55, 57–62, 64, 67, 71

impact, 5–7, 11, 12, 17, 46–48, 58, 61, 62, 71
implementation, 19, 39
importance, 3, 4, 9, 11, 12, 14, 17, 26, 28, 38, 44, 48, 59, 71, 72
imprisonment, 20
improvement, 44
inability, 2
inception, 15
inclusion, 27, 49, 71
inclusivity, 14, 15, 28, 35, 37, 39, 41, 43, 44, 46, 49, 59, 61, 62
increase, 68
individual, 3, 17, 23, 39, 62, 71
inequality, 1, 8, 39, 40
influence, 8, 11, 14, 17, 19, 48
information, 11, 17, 38
initiative, 61, 62
injustice, 41
inspiration, 71
instance, 8, 10, 14, 20, 34, 36, 39, 43
interconnectedness, 72
interplay, 1, 13, 15, 17, 21, 26, 35, 37, 48, 55, 57, 59
intersection, 8, 20, 38
intersectionality, 2, 5, 7, 9, 10, 12, 14, 19, 20, 24, 27, 28, 31, 37–39, 44, 58, 60, 62, 64, 67, 72
involvement, 59
isolation, 8, 59

job, 48
John Rawls, 33
journey, 26, 35, 37, 43, 59, 62
Judith Butler's, 24
justice, 7, 15, 24, 33–35, 37–39, 41–43, 46, 48, 49, 64, 67,

Index

72

Karl Marx, 40
Kimberlé Crenshaw, 10, 19, 20, 24, 38, 58
knowledge, 38

lack, 11, 36, 54, 55, 59
landscape, 2, 13, 16, 17, 19, 24, 25, 27, 29, 41, 46, 48, 55, 58, 62, 70, 71
leadership, 46
legacy, 17, 26, 62
legislation, 11, 46
lens, 1, 7, 15, 19, 20, 24, 60, 64
life, 4, 47
light, 53
living, 35
loss, 58

mainstream, 47
making, 21, 48, 54, 67
management, 55, 57
march, 21
marginalization, 1, 20, 59
Marx, 40
matter, 67
meaning, 59
means, 14, 59, 70
meeting, 66
memory, 14, 37–39
microcosm, 36
misinformation, 11, 28
mobilization, 17
model, 31, 35, 46
momentum, 16
motto, 21
movement, 5, 7, 15, 18, 22–24, 29, 72
multiplicity, 10

myriad, 27
myth, 13

narrative, 1, 13–15, 17, 20, 21, 39, 59, 67
nation, 17
nature, 3, 10, 12, 22, 40, 41, 45
necessity, 10, 14, 15, 21, 35, 55
need, 12, 21, 27, 39, 41, 43, 45, 46, 61, 64, 70
negotiation, 59
non, 4, 21, 38
normalization, 11
nourishment, 37

one, 28, 33, 58
opposition, 35
oppression, 1, 3, 8, 10, 15, 17, 19–22, 24, 29, 61, 62, 64
order, 55, 66, 68
organization, 17, 21, 59
organizing, 11, 21, 27
orientation, 10, 20, 42, 47
origin, 13, 15
ostracism, 4
other, 26, 28, 31, 71, 72
outrage, 27
outreach, 43
overlap, 10

parade, 18
parity, 33
participation, 49
past, 12, 58, 61
people, 15, 27, 38, 55
perception, 11
performance, 21
performativity, 24
person, 39
perspective, 58, 60, 61

phenomenon, 19, 46
philosopher, 41
planning, 27
platform, 47
play, 20
plight, 18
point, 67
policy, 7, 11, 12, 48
pool, 38
population, 17, 18, 34, 54, 55, 61
portrayal, 11, 21
positioning, 8
post, 2, 4, 53, 57–62, 64, 65, 67, 70
potential, 3, 7, 29, 39, 40, 61, 64
power, 5, 7, 11, 13, 15, 17, 21, 31, 49, 57, 61, 70, 71
practicality, 41
practice, 36, 40
precedent, 71
pressure, 39
pride, 18, 21, 47
privilege, 8, 38
process, 44, 55, 57, 59–61, 71
programming, 46
progress, 23, 24, 26, 44, 48, 49
promise, 41
promotion, 62
propaganda, 17
protest, 18
public, 11, 21, 38, 43, 47, 71
purpose, 30, 37, 58, 59
pursuit, 7, 35, 37, 39, 41

quest, 26, 70
quo, 40

race, 10, 20, 24, 58
racism, 8, 27
Rawls, 33

reality, 1, 55
realization, 36
rebirth, 13
rebuilding, 2, 55, 61, 62, 64, 71
recognition, 2, 4, 10, 15, 17, 21, 22, 26, 37, 42, 55, 61, 64, 66, 67, 69–71
reconstruction, 60, 70
recovery, 55, 57, 62, 64, 67
redefinition, 59
refuge, 65
regime, 17, 21
regression, 55, 67
relation, 55
relationship, 11, 19, 21, 53
relief, 67
remembering, 57
reminder, 35, 37, 57
renewal, 62
report, 59, 71
representation, 11, 12, 14, 15, 27, 28, 43, 46, 47
resilience, 4, 7, 11–13, 15–17, 19, 21, 23, 24, 26, 29–31, 35, 38, 44, 46, 48, 50, 55, 57, 59, 60, 62, 64, 67, 70, 71
resistance, 7, 16, 17, 19, 21, 34, 35, 48, 61, 64
resource, 53, 55, 57, 59, 65, 66
respect, 42
response, 1, 8, 10, 14, 16, 54, 58, 61
responsibility, 66
restructuring, 14
result, 13, 55, 58
resurgence, 71
retribution, 61
rise, 48
risk, 21

Index

role, 2, 3, 5, 10, 12, 14, 30, 37–39, 55, 61, 62, 66, 71
rupture, 55

s, 4, 15, 17–19, 21, 24, 27, 29, 35, 39–41, 44–46, 53, 55, 57–59, 61, 68
safety, 13, 21, 55, 65
scarcity, 61, 66, 71
section, 3, 5, 10, 19, 22, 29, 39, 42, 46, 55, 58, 62, 67
self, 58
sense, 4, 11, 14, 30, 37, 38, 44, 47–50, 58, 59, 61, 67
series, 13, 24
setting, 58
sex, 20, 46
sexuality, 20, 58
shape, 3, 4, 35, 48
share, 14, 21, 28, 47, 50, 59, 71
sharing, 59, 61, 65, 66
shift, 16
significance, 60
society, 1, 2, 4, 8, 11, 13–15, 17, 19, 22, 24, 33, 35, 37, 39–42, 44, 46, 48, 53, 55, 58, 59, 62, 64–67, 70, 71
socio, 2, 17, 20, 27, 29, 62
solidarity, 10, 11, 18, 26, 29–31, 48, 50, 54, 57, 59, 61, 64, 66, 67, 71
space, 39
spectacle, 21
spectrum, 38
spirit, 21, 35
stability, 53, 58
stance, 43
state, 18, 21, 37, 41
status, 20, 40

stigma, 17, 45
story, 13, 15
storytelling, 57, 61, 71
strategy, 65
strength, 29, 48
structuralism, 58
structure, 15, 24, 33
struggle, 2, 9, 14, 15, 19, 26, 35, 41, 58, 61, 64, 65, 67, 71
study, 10
sum, 39
summary, 21, 26, 35, 55
Sundering, 13, 14
support, 4, 11, 13, 21, 23, 31, 35, 43, 50, 58, 59, 61, 65–67, 71
surveillance, 17
survival, 1, 4, 14, 55, 57–59, 61, 64–67, 71
survivor, 59
sword, 28
symbol, 21
system, 1, 37, 38

tapestry, 26
target, 20
technology, 11, 12
television, 21
tenet, 14
tension, 39, 41, 61
term, 14, 20, 50, 55
testament, 15, 17, 21, 57, 59, 61, 70
theme, 10, 11, 17, 59
theory, 5, 7, 15, 19, 20, 24, 33, 38, 60, 62, 67
thinking, 37
Thomas More, 35
Thomas More,, 40
thought, 39, 41
threat, 48, 61

tool, 10, 14, 17, 57, 59, 71
tradition, 14
transgender, 38
transphobia, 48
trauma, 13, 58, 59
treatment, 71
trial, 21

underpinning, 33, 67
understanding, 3, 9, 10, 12, 13, 38, 40, 47, 58, 61, 71
unity, 14, 29–31, 48
urgency, 30
utopia, 35–37, 40, 42
utopianism, 41

vigilance, 35, 44, 46
violence, 20, 24, 48, 54, 55, 64, 65, 68, 71

visibility, 11, 47
vision, 2, 36–41
vulnerability, 61

wake, 15
war, 17
way, 48
web, 8
well, 41, 65
whole, 14
work, 22, 31, 44
world, 5, 13, 14, 59

Xylon, 1, 4, 8, 10–31

youth, 43

Zephyria, 1, 35, 36, 40, 41
Zephyrian, 43